Mountain Biking
Boise

Martin Potucek

FALCON® Helena, Montana

*A*FALCONGUIDE®

Falcon® Publishing is continually expanding its list of recreational guide-books. All books include detailed descriptions, accurate maps, and all information necessary for enjoyable trips. You can order extra copies of this book and get information and prices for other Falcon® books by writing Falcon, P.O. Box 1718, Helena, MT 59624, or by calling toll-free 1-800-582-2665. Also, please ask for a copy of our current catalog. Visit our website at www.Falcon.com or contact us by e-mail at falcon@falcon.com.

©1998 by Falcon® Publishing Co. Inc., Helena, Montana.
Printed in Canada.

2 3 4 5 6 7 8 9 10 TP 05 04 03 02 01 00

Falcon and FalconGuide are registered trademarks of Falcon® Publishing, Inc.

Cover photo by Glenn Oakley.

Library of Congress Cataloging in Publication Data.
Potucek, Martin, 1950-
        Mountain biking Boise / by Martin Potucek.
            p.   cm.
        Includes bibliographical references (p.) and index.
        ISBN 1-56044-599-8 (paperback)
        1. All terrain cycling—Idaho—Boise Region—Guidebooks.
    2. Bicycle trails—Idaho—Boise Region—Guidebooks. 3. Boise Region
    (Idaho)—Guidebooks. I. Title.
    GV1045.5.I252B657   1998
    917.96'28—dc21
                                                            97-44038
                                                                CIP

CAUTION

Outdoor recreational activities are by their very nature potentially hazardous. All participants in such activities must assume the responsibility for their own actions and safety. The information contained in this guidebook cannot replace sound judgment and good decision-making skills, which help reduce the risk exposure, nor does the scope of this book allow for disclosure of all the potential hazards and risks involved in such activities.

Learn as much as possible about the outdoor recreational activities in which you participate, prepare for the unexpected, and be cautious. The reward will be a safer and more enjoyable experience.

 Text pages printed on recycled paper.

Contents

Acknowledgments

Over the space of eighteen months and 1,500 miles, this book took on a life of its own. Although most of my time on the trails was spent solo, I'm indebted to a number of people, offices, and agencies for their help in putting this book together.

There is a sense of stewardship of the land in the Boise area shared by a community of technicians, engineers, strollers, rollers, rockers, landowners, bikers, and officials. In spite of the wide spectrum of agendas represented by these various groups, it is remarkable how cohesive the sentiments are and how well Boise and its Front are managed.

Tim Breuer, Ridge to Rivers Trails Coordinator, along with others at the BLM (especially the women who run the map room) were essential to pointing me in the right direction.

Dave Selvage, Parks Planner with the Boise Parks and Recreation Department, was instrumental in setting me straight about the location and interplay of private and city properties. In a rapidly expanding town such as Boise, that information proved invaluable, not only in outlining the present, but in projecting what is in progess, as well.

Lew Peterson has been most helpful with maps and information on the recent blaze of goings-on at Bogus Basin Ski Resort. Watch for more to come in the summer up there.

Jake Hawkes of Moo Cycles was excellent in giving energetic and forthright (if not always kosher) descriptions of new trails.

My thanks go to Ron Dillon for his connections to others with intimate knowledge of the area (such as Dan Meeker). Ron's hosting of the Nike Wild Rockies Mountain Bike Series is a great asset for the promotion of the sport (especially races and special events) in this area and across the Northwest.

David Law-Smith and Ross Nickerson at Boise State University were also helpful in giving good advice and keeping me on-line.

Richard B. Smith (yes, the name you see all over the North End on real estate signs) was warm and gracious with his detailed information on and history of the foothills and his thoughtful consideration of its future.

Georgia Meacham was good for a push when I lost the Oregon Trail at Columbia Village and needed not only directions, but details and connections.

Thanks to the staffs of the Boise City Library and the Albertson Library at Boise State University for helping me find the right tools. And to the folks at the Boise Front office of the Boise National Forest and the Barber Park office in Ada County, who were all helpful and forthcoming with much-needed information about the Old Pen.

And had it not been for the patience, understanding, and the occasional thump to the brain from my family, this book would never be.

Martin Potucek
Boise, Idaho
November, 1997

MAP LEGEND

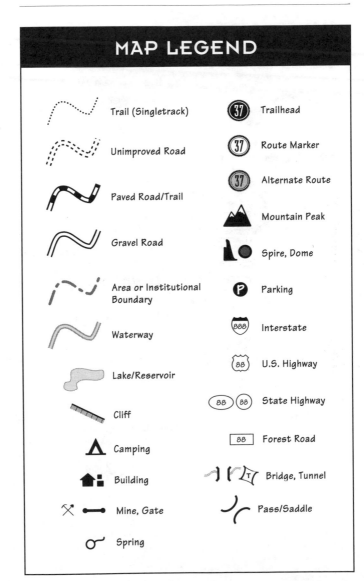

Trail (Singletrack)

Unimproved Road

Paved Road/Trail

Gravel Road

Area or Institutional Boundary

Waterway

Lake/Reservoir

Cliff

Camping

Building

Mine, Gate

Spring

Trailhead

Route Marker

Alternate Route

Mountain Peak

Spire, Dome

Parking

Interstate

U.S. Highway

State Highway

Forest Road

Bridge, Tunnel

Pass/Saddle

BOISE AREA

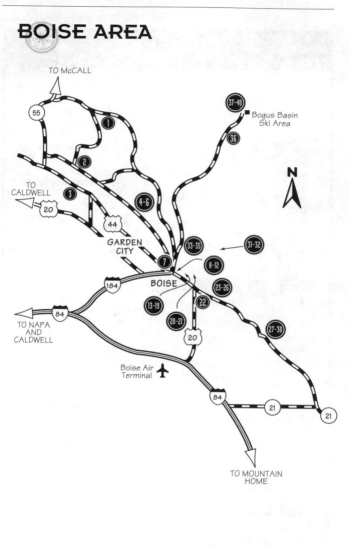

TO McCALL

55

1

2

TO CALDWELL

20

3

44

4-6

GARDEN CITY

7

184

BOISE

13-19

20-21

20

TO NAPA AND CALDWELL

84

Boise Air Terminal

84

21

21

33-35

31-32

8-12

23-26

22

27-30

37-40

Bogus Basin Ski Area

36

N

TO MOUNTAIN HOME

USGS 7.5 MINUTE MAPS, BOISE AREA

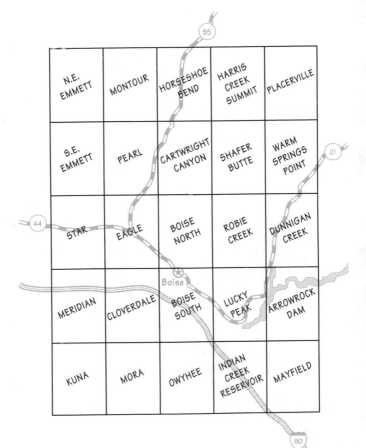

		55		
N.E. EMMETT	MONTOUR	HORSESHOE BEND	HARRIS CREEK SUMMIT	PLACERVILLE
S.E. EMMETT	PEARL	CARTWRIGHT CANYON	SHAFER BUTTE	WARM SPRINGS POINT
STAR	EAGLE	BOISE NORTH	ROBIE CREEK	DUNNIGAN CREEK
MERIDIAN	CLOVERDALE	BOISE SOUTH	LUCKY PEAK	ARROWROCK DAM
KUNA	MORA	OWYHEE	INDIAN CREEK RESERVOIR	MAYFIELD

Get Ready to CRANK!

Welcome to Boise. Here are forty rides ranging from easy road routes to sub-alpine technical ascents. The rides are all loops, beginning and ending in the same place, and are described in plain language, with accurate distances and ratings for physical and technical difficulty. Each entry offers detailed information that is easy to read and use, from armchair or trailside.

Whether you are a local sprockethead, an intermediate wanting to improve your range and skill, or just someone looking for an easier or different ride, this book is written for you.

The aim of this guide is threefold: to help you choose a ride that is appropriate for your fitness and skill level; to make it easy for you to find the trailhead; and to help you complete the ride safely, without getting lost.

All of the rides in this guide are accessible by bicycle from downtown Boise, although you may want to drive to the trailhead for outlying rides like those at Bogus Basin Ski Area.

These basics are the tools to open your world, benefitting from the experience (mistakes) of others. For more than twenty years now, a small but growing community of multi-users (hikers, bikers, and horse-back riders) have cooperated to keep the foothills and their higher reaches open and accessible. This book operates on this ethic: With these tools (this knowledge) comes the responsibilty to travel safely, prudently, and to respect the rights of others, whether they are landowners, lizards, or lichens.

There is a community in the Boise area that shares the same urges: to discover and travel the terrain lightly and quickly, without leaving a trace. We have seen a huge wave of support (even from the larger community of Boise itself) rise and focus after the damage caused by the 8th Street Fire of August, 1996.

According to local lore, the fire was started by an off-duty police officer who was shooting tracer bullets at the firing range, up the hill from the military reserve building. Within thirty-six hours the conflagration had reached the Boise Ridge, burning 15,000 acres before it was snuffed.

Since then a massive community, state, and federal effort has been launched to mitigate the effects of the fire with contour trenches, holding ponds, etc. These measures have been controversial, especially since the flash flood of September, 1997, wiped out Lower Hull's Gulch (Trail 29) and Bob's Trail (Lower Crane Creek, Trail 30).

Please consider these facts when traveling in the gulches. A system of rotating sirens has been installed across the lower foothills. If you are out there, especially in a low-lying area, and you hear the sirens, you should get to high ground immediately. The sirens are tested for thirty seconds, at noon, on the first Saturday of every month. In an emergency, the sirens will sound for three minutes, except for the sirens at the end of 36th Street North and Bob's Trail (#30), which chime nine times in sequence.

The Boise Front: What to Expect

The rides in this book cover a wide variety of terrain. From the Boise River greenbelt, where a variety of multi-users thread in and out of each other's paths, to trails rising thousands of feet on rock and sand, the Boise area offers a wide spectrum of fat-tire rides.

Although the Boise Front (the southern spine of the Boise Range which "fronts" Boise itself) may not present the rugged, true-alpine conditions that characterizes some areas, its ease of access to the Boise Ridge (the summit ridge that extends from Boise Peak northward) via a well developed system of public and private trails, makes it an exceptional area for the recreational mountain biker. Smooth pavement to world-class-obstacles are found here in close proximity.

Mountain terrain requires preparedness. Know your equipment, and know your abilities. This book is not intended as a primer or guide to the sport of mountain biking; it's a guide to specific rides with specific conditions that are, however, changing constantly. Those starting out should try the shorter, easier routes, and then, as conditioning and skills improve, reach for the longer, more difficult rides. Readiness can only be measured by your own level of confidence.

Whatever your motivation for biking is, this book is written with the following premise: that biking should be non-competitive and non-egocentric; the thrill of the experience lies between the terrain and you. All else is distraction and window dressing; it doesn't matter what generation lycra you wear or whether you are fully suspended. When pumping that sustained steep hill or preparing to launch some precipice, chill your jets—take a look around—and appreciate the moment.

Boise's weather is relatively benign and sunny, but as you travel higher out of the valley, precipitation and temperatures become more extreme. The greatest disparity of conditions is presented by the Boise River and Bogus Basin Ski Area, representing almost 5,000 vertical feet of change in 10 miles. When it's wet, the best places to ride are down low (Boise's elevation is about 2,700 feet), and when it's hot, the Boise ridge is a welcome getaway.

Most of the good off-road riding in the Boise vicinity happens from mid-May through October. Trails at higher elevations have even shorter seasons, running from late June through September. Some trails are closed from January to April to protect wintering deer and elk; these restrictions are noted for each ride and are generally located on the lower to middle reaches of Shaw Mountain.

At any time of year rain or snow can turn trails into a purée that lasts for days. Please stay off wet, muddy trails. The risk of soil damage and erosion is simply too great. A good rule of thumb: if you leave a track, don't go.

"POSTED: NO TRESPASSING!"

Boise is lucky to have some of the best mountain biking in Idaho right out its back door. Table Rock, Military Reserve, and Bogus Basin are home to a maze of classic double- and singletrack rides all within a bunny hop of downtown.

But this maze features more than its share of deadends— "no trespassing" signs and barbed wire fences strung across trails. Sadly, new deadends crop up every season, closing once-popular trails and, in some cases, blocking access to public lands beyond.

A glance at the Boise National Forest Visitor Map reveals the scope of the problem. If the trails are a maze, the lands they cross are a jigsaw puzzle of public and private ownership. Take out the private pieces of the puzzle and the maze cannot be unriddled from start to finish.

Similar situations are also found in the Snake River Canyon, along sections of the Oregon Trail, and along the Boise River.

Many of the private holdings are old mining claims—strips and odd-shaped scraps that ignore topography in favor of following hoped-for veins of wealth below ground. Today these parcels are prospected for their value as home sites, and the owners are growing ever more cautious about who goes traipsing across their investments. Where people have recently built homes, they typically close old trails to keep the public off their new backyards. That's their prerogative: public access to private land is a privilege, not a right. We should thank the many landowners who have allowed access for so many years.

But what the current trend means to us mountain bikers (and hikers, runners, and horseback riders) is that our local trail network is shrinking. Lydle Gulch has long been private property, but only since 1994 have its trails been posted against trespassing.

In fact, 24 of the 40 rides described in this book cross private property. Public access on these trails depends upon a good relationship between landowners and users. In short, it's the reader's responsibility to determine whether the trails—even those described on the following pages—are open or not.

In a few cases landowners have informally allowed access as long as trail users don't cause any problems. Other landowners grant use of the trails on an individual basis when cyclists ask permission ahead of time. And more widespread efforts are being made to acquire easements and rights-of-way (or even to buy land outright) by several conservation groups, hoping to raise funds through bond issues for buying land in and around town to set aside for viewsheds and recreation and working to secure other lands and access in areas throughout the region, both to preserve plant and wildlife habitat and to provide recreational opportunities. For more information on these and other groups, see the addresses in Appendix B.

In the meantime, all trail users should follow a few rules of common courtesy (and Idaho law):

• Ask permission first to enter or cross private property. Check at the local bike shops or the County Assessor's Office (see Appendix B) for land ownership information.

• Familiarize yourself with Idaho's trespass law, particularly Idaho code sections 18-7008, 18-7011, 6-202, 6-202A, and 5-218. According to the law, you can enter private land only with explicit permission from the landowner. The posting requirements are simple: written notice (a sign) or 100 square inches of orange paint on a post, structure, or natural object. If property is posted, no one is allowed access without permission from the landowner.

• Respect all property, private or public. Leave all gates as you find them. Do not damage fences or other facilities, and avoid spooking livestock.

• Strive to be inconspicuous. Ride quietly and in small groups. Prevent erosion: do not skid or ride when trails are wet and muddy. Stay on designated trails and roads. Check your bike and clothing for seeds and weeds to prevent the spread of noxious plants. Knapweed and goathead thorns are common around Boise; knapweed is easily snagged in chains and pedals; goatheads stick to clothes and tires. Do not litter.

• Wear a helmet and ride in control at all times. Landowners and managers are less skittish about mountain bikers when we take responsibility for our own safety. If you do get hurt, don't blame the landowner.

• If you meet the landowner while on the property, be friendly and honest. You are an ambassador for all riders who follow. Some landowners see mountain bikers as a liability risk—"What if a biker crashes and gets hurt on my land? Will he or she sue me?" You can reassure them by taking time to talk with them as any reasonable person would (but please don't show off your chainring scars and missing teeth). Some folks know about Idaho's recreation access law Idaho code sections 36-1601 through 36-1604, which limits the liability of landowners who allow free use of their property for recreation. Mention this if it seems appropriate to the conversation. And take every opportunity to thank the landowner for allowing access to his or her property.

Finally, consider joining one of the local groups working to preserve trails and land access. Chip in when they hold a work day to repair and maintain trails, pull weeds, or pick up trash. Pay membership dues in lieu of joining a health club, and then get your workout on the trails you've helped protect. Become more involved in helping city and county officials plan and develop local open space opportunities. In short, be an all-around advocate for trails.

Rules of the Trail

If every mountain biker always yielded the right-of-way, stayed on the trail, avoided wet or muddy trails, never cut switchbacks, never skidded, always rode in control, showed respect for other trail users, and carried out every last scrap of what was carried in (candy wrappers and bike-part debris included)—in short, *did the right thing*—then we wouldn't need a list of rules governing our behavior.

Most of us don't need rules. But we do need knowledge. What exactly *is* the right thing to do?

Here are some guidelines—I like to think of them as re-minders—reprinted by permission from the International Mountain Bicycling Association (IMBA). The basic theme here is to reduce or eliminate any damage to the land and water, the

plant and wildlife inhabitants, and other backcountry visitors and trail users. Ride with respect.

IMBA Rules of the Trail

1. Ride on open trails only. Respect trail and road closures (ask if not sure), avoid possible trespass on private land, obtain permits and authorization as may be required. Federal and state wilderness areas are closed to cycling. The way you ride will influence trail management decisions and policies.

2. Zero Impact. Be sensitive to the dirt beneath you. Even on open (legal) trails, you should not ride under conditions where you will leave evidence of your passing, such as on certain soils after a rain. Recognize different types of soil and trail construction; practice low-impact cycling. This also means staying on existing trails and not creating any new ones. Be sure to pack out at least as much as you pack in.

3. Control your bicycle! Inattention for even a second can cause problems. Obey all bicycle speed regulations and recommendations.

4. Always yield trail. Make known your approach well in advance. A friendly greeting (or bell) is considerate and works well; don't startle others. Show your respect when passing by slowing to a walking pace or even stopping. Anticipate other trail users around corners or in blind spots.

5. Never spook animals. All animals are startled by an unannounced approach, a sudden movement, or a loud noise. This can be dangerous for you, others, and the animals. Give animals extra room and time to adjust to you. When passing horses, use special care and follow directions from the horseback riders (ask if uncertain). Running cattle and disturbing wildlife is a serious offense. Leave gates as you found them, or as marked.

6. Plan ahead. Know your equipment, your ability, and the area in which you are riding—and prepare accordingly. Be self-sufficient at all times, keep your equipment in good repair, and carry necessary supplies for changes in weather or other conditions. A well-executed trip is a satisfaction to you and not a burden or offense to others. Always wear a helmet.

Keep trails open by setting a good example of environmentally sound and socially responsible off-road cycling. For more information, contact:

Jim Hasenauer, Director of Education, IMBA,
e-mail: IMBAJim@aol.com

How to Use this Guide

Mountain Biking Boise describes forty mountain bike rides in their entirety. A handful of other local routes are mentioned briefly in Appendix A.

All of the featured rides are loops, beginning and ending at the same point. Loops are by far the most popular type of ride, and Boiseans are lucky to have so many so close to home. Be forewarned, however: the difficulty of a loop ride may change dramatically depending on which direction you ride around the loop. If you are unfamiliar with the rides in this book, try them first as described here. The directions follow the path of least resistance (which does not necessarily mean "easy"). After you've been over the terrain, you can determine whether a given loop would be fun—or even feasible—in the reverse direction.

Portions of some rides follow gravel and even paved roads, and a handful of rides never wander off road. Purists may wince at road rides in a book about mountain biking, but these are special rides. They offer a chance to enjoy mountain scenery and fresh air while covering easier, non-technical terrain ideal for people new to the sport. They can also be used by hardcore riders on "active rest" days or when higher elevation trails are closed by mud or snow.

Each ride description in this book follows the same format:

Number and Name of the Ride: Rides are cross referenced by number throughout this book. In many cases, parts of rides or entire routes can be linked to other rides for longer trips or variations on a standard route.

For the names of rides I relied on official names of trails, roads, and natural features as shown on national forest and U.S. Geological Survey maps. In some cases long-time, local names are used (especially when they're used by the Ridge to Rivers Trail System) or are referred to in passing.

Location: The general whereabouts of the ride; distance and direction from Boise.

Distance: The length of the ride in miles, given as a loop or round trip.

Time: An estimate of how long it takes to complete the ride— for example: one to two hours. *The time listed is the actual riding time and does not include rest stops.* Strong, skilled riders may be able to do a given ride in less than the estimated time, while other riders may take considerably longer. Also bear in mind that severe weather, changes in trail conditions, or mechanical problems may prolong a ride.

Tread: The type of road or trail: paved road, gravel road, dirt road or jeep track, doubletrack, or singletrack.

Aerobic level: The level of physical effort required to complete the ride: easy, moderate, or strenuous. (See the explanation of the rating systems on page 13).

Technical difficulty: The level of bike handling skills needed to complete the ride upright and in one piece. Technical difficulty is rated on a scale from 1 to 5, with 1 being the easiest and 5 the hardest (see the explanation of the rating systems on page 13).

Hazards: A list of dangers that may be encountered on a ride, including traffic, weather, trail obstacles and conditions, risky stream crossings, difficult route-finding, and other perils. Remember that conditions may change at any time. Be alert for storms, new fences, downfall, missing trail signs, and mechanical failure. Fatigue, heat, cold, and/or dehydration may impair judgment. Always wear a helmet and other safety equipment. Ride in control at all times.

Highlights: Special features or qualities that make a ride worth doing: scenery, fun singletrack, chances to see wildlife (as if we needed an excuse!).

Land status: A list of managing agencies and private inholdings. Most of the rides in this book are on Bureau of Land Management, Boise National Forest, and Idaho state lands. But many of the rides also cross portions of private or municipal lands. Always leave gates as you found them. And respect the land, regardless of who owns it. See Appendix B for a list of local addresses for land-managing agencies.

Maps: A list of available maps. The Boise National Forest visitors' map and the Ridge to Rivers Trail System map afford a good overview of travel routes in the region. USGS topographic maps in the 7.5-minute quad series provide a close-up look at terrain. Also, the Bureau of Land Management 1:100,000 map for Boise shows topography and many travel routes for the area. Not all routes are shown on official maps. Trail numbers and letters used in this guide refer to the Ridge to Rivers Trail System designations; most of the trails in this book are marked at key junctions by these signs (usually a brown fiberglass stake).

Access: How to find the trailhead or the start of the ride. Most rides can be pedaled right from town; for others it is best to drive to the trailhead.

The ride: A mile-by-mile list of key points—landmarks, notable climbs and descents, stream crossings, obstacles, hazards, major turns and junctions—along the ride. All distances were measured to the tenth of a mile with a cyclo-computer (a bike-mounted odometer). Terrain, riding technique, and even tire pressure can affect odometer readings, so treat all mileages as estimates.

Finally, one last reminder that the real world is changing all the time. The information presented here is as accurate and up-to-date as possible, but there are no guarantees out in the mountains. You alone are responsible for your safety and for the choices you make on the trail.

If you do find an error or omission in this book, or a new and noteworthy change in the field, I'd like to hear from you. Please write to Martin Potucek, c/o Falcon Publishing, P.O. Box 1718, Helena, MT 59624.

Rating the Rides—One Person's Pain is Another's Pleasure

Falcon's mountain biking guides rate each ride for two types of difficulty: the *physical effort* required to pedal the distance, and the level of *bike-handling skills* needed to stay upright and make it home in one piece. We call these **Aerobic level** and **Technical difficulty.**

The following sections explain what the various ratings mean in plain, specific language. An elevation profile accompanies each ride description to help you determine how easy or hard the ride is. You should also weigh other factors such as elevation above sea level, total trip distance, weather and wind, and current trail conditions.

Aerobic Level Ratings

Bicycling is often touted as a relaxing, low-impact, relatively easy way to burn excess calories and maintain a healthy heart and lungs. Mountain biking, however, tends to pack a little more work (and excitement) into the routine.

Fat tires and soft or rough trails increase the rolling resistance, so it takes more effort to push those wheels around.

Unpaved or off-road hills tend to be steeper than grades measured and surfaced by the highway department. When we use the word *steep*, we mean a sweat-inducing, oxygen-sucking, lactose-building climb. If it is followed by an exclamation point—steep !—expect some honest pain on the way up (and maybe for days afterward).

So expect to breathe hard and sweat some, probably a lot. Pedaling around town is a good start, but it won't fully prepare you for the workout offered by most of the rides in this book. If you are unsure of your level of fitness, see a doctor for a physical exam before tackling any of the rides in this book. And if you are riding to get back in shape or just for the fun of it, take it easy. Walk or rest if need be. Start with short rides and add on miles gradually.

Here's how we rate the exertion level for terrain covered in this book:

Easy: Flat or gently rolling terrain. No steep or prolonged climbs.

Moderate: Some hills. Climbs may be short and fairly steep or long and gradual.

Strenuous: Frequent or prolonged climbs steep enough to require riding in the lowest gear; requires a high level of aerobic fitness, power, and endurance (typically acquired through many hours of riding and proper training). Less fit riders may need to walk.

Many rides are mostly easy and moderate but may have short strenuous sections. Other rides are mostly strenuous and should be attempted only after a complete medical checkup and implant of a second heart, preferably a *big* one. Also be aware that flailing through a highly technical section can be exhausting even on the flats. Good riding skills and a relaxed stance on the bike save energy.

Finally, any ride can be strenuous if you ride it hard and fast. Conversely, the pain of a lung-burning climb grows easier to tolerate as your fitness level improves. Learn to pace yourself and remember to schedule easy rides and rest days into your calendar.

Elevation Profiles

An elevation profile accompanies each ride description. Here the ups and downs of the route are graphed on a grid of elevation (in feet above sea level) on the left and miles pedaled across the bottom. Route surface conditions (see map legend) and technical levels are shown on the graphs.

Note that these graphs are compressed (squeezed) to fit on the page. The actual slopes you will ride are not as steep as the lines drawn on the graphs (it just feels that way). Also, some extremely short dips and climbs are too small to show up on the graphs. All such abrupt changes in gradient are, however, mentioned in the mile-by-mile ride description.

Technical Difficulty Ratings

While you are pushing up that steep, strenuous slope, wondering how much farther you can go before you collapse, remember that the condition of your heart, lungs, and legs aren't the only factors that affect the way to the top of the mountain.

There's that tree across the trail, or the sideslope full of ball-bearing sized pebbles, or the place where the trail disappears except for faint bits of rubber clinging to a boulder the size of your garage.

Mountain bikes will roll over or through an amazing array of challenges, but sometimes we, as riders, have to help. And, even more astonishing, some riders get off their bikes and walk—get this—*before* they flip over the handlebars.

The technical difficulty ratings in this book help take the worst surprises out of backcountry rides. In the privacy of your own home you can make an honest appraisal of your bike-handling skills and then find rides in these pages that are within your ability.

We rate technical difficulty on a scale from 1 to 5, from easiest to most difficult. We tried to make the ratings as objective as possible by considering the type of obstacles and their frequency of occurrence. The same standards were applied consistently through all the rides in this book.

We've also added plus (+) and minus (-) symbols to cover gray areas between given levels of difficulty: a 4+ obstacle is harder than a 4, but easier than a 5-. A stretch of trail rated 5+ would be unrideable by all but the most skilled (or luckiest) riders.

Here are the five levels defined:

Level 1: Smooth tread; road or doubletrack; no obstacles, ruts, or steeps. Requires basic bike riding skills.

Level 2: Mostly smooth tread; wide, well-groomed singletrack or road/doubletrack with minor ruts or loose gravel or sand.

Level 3: Irregular tread with some rough sections; single or doubletrack with obvious route choices; some steep sections; occasional obstacles may include small rocks, roots, water bars, ruts, loose gravel or sand, and sharp turns or broad, open switchbacks.

Level 4: Rough tread with few smooth places; singletrack or rough doubletrack with limited route choices; steep sections, some with obstacles; obstacles are numerous and varied, including rocks, roots, branches, ruts, sidehills, narrow tread, loose gravel or sand, and switchbacks.

Level 5: Continuously broken, rocky, root-infested, or trenched tread; singletrack or extremely rough doubletrack with few route choices; frequent, sudden, and severe changes in gradient; some slopes so steep that wheels lift off ground; obstacles are nearly continuous and may include boulders, logs, water, large holes, deep ruts, ledges, piles of loose gravel, steep sidehills, encroaching trees, and tight switchbacks.

Again, most of the rides in this book cover varied terrain, with an ever-changing degree of technical difficulty. Some trails run smooth with only occasional obstacles, and other trails are seemingly all obstacle. The path of least resistance, or *line*, is where you find it. In general, most obstacles are more challenging if you encounter them while climbing than while descending. On the other hand, in heavy surf (e.g., boulder fields, tangles of downfall, cliffs), fear plays a larger role when facing downhill.

Realize, too, that different riders have different strengths and weaknesses. Some folks can scramble over logs and boulders without a grunt, but they crash head over heels on every switchback turn. Some fly off the steepest drops and others freeze. Some riders climb like the wind and others just blow— and walk.

The key to overcoming "technical difficulties" is practice: keep trying. Follow a rider who makes it look easy, and don't hesitate to ask for constructive criticism. Try shifting your weight (good riders move a lot, front to back, side to side, and up and down), and experiment with balance and momentum. Find a smooth patch of lawn and practice riding as slowly as possible, even balancing at a standstill in a "track stand" (described in the Glossary). This will give you more confidence— and more time to recover or bail out—the next time the trail rears up and bites.

Hidden Springs Loop

Location: Northwest Boise foothills.

Distance: 6.3 miles.

Time: 40 to 60 minutes.

Tread: 2.1 miles on gravel; 1 mile on jeep road; and 3.2 miles of singletrack.

Aerobic level: Moderate.

Technical difficulty: 1 to 2 on roads; 2 to 3+ on trails.

Hazards: Gravel the size of peas and marbles; fast-approaching clouds of dust (with cars in them) on county roads; tricky soft spots on trails; goathead thorns at the trailhead and lining the county roads.

Highlights: Complete with bridge, drains, basalt gardens, and a rocky, pedestrian-only loop, this trail system introduces an area that used to be off limits to bikers; and is a good example of the good that results from community effort. A glance up at looming Stack Rock gives an idea of the terrain potential of this western arm of the Boise Front.

Land status: Public roads; trails are a public/private cooperative effort. The Hidden Springs development has allowed access for most of this loop; their plan and its final implementation will have a huge impact on the future design of the foothills.

Maps: USGS Boise North, Eagle; Boise National Forest, BLM Boise Front, Ridge to Rivers.

HIDDEN SPRINGS LOOP
Ride 1

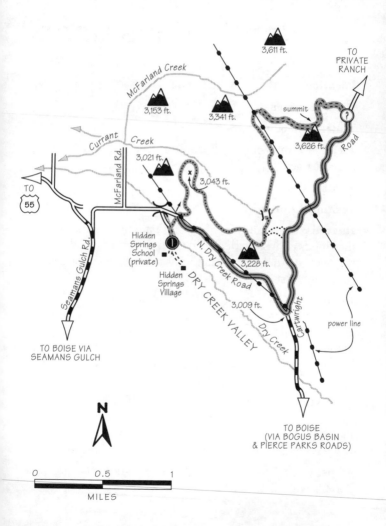

McFarland Creek

3,611 ft.

3,153 ft.

3,341 ft.

summit

3,626 ft.

TO
PRIVATE
RANCH

Road

Currant   Creek

3,021 ft.

3,043 ft.

McFarland Rd.

TO
55

Seamans Gulch Rd.

Hidden
Springs School
(private)

Hidden
Springs
Village

N. Dry Creek Road

DRY CREEK VALLEY

3,228 ft.

3,009 ft.

Dry Creek

Cartwright

power line

TO BOISE VIA
SEAMANS GULCH

TO BOISE
(VIA BOGUS BASIN
& PIERCE PARKS ROADS)

N

0   0.5   1
MILES

Access: From Boise go to the intersection of Dry Creek Road (paved) and Dry Creek Road North (gravel) via Highway 55 North (about 5 miles north of State Street), or by going up Seamans Gulch Road north off of Hill Road. Go out Dry Creek North. Just before crossing Dry Creek, turn right on the road that parallels Dry Creek. In 0.3 mile, you will come to the parking area at the new Hidden Springs Village. The ride starts here.

The Ride:

0.0   From the parking lot, you will see a footbridge over Dry Creek. Cross it and proceed through a meadow via a sandy, gravel singletrack.

0.2   Cross North Dry Creek Road and head up a new dirt singletrack that climbs moderately, to the right (southeast).

0.6   Sidehill left under a small saddle which loops around a ridge.

0.9   At a small saddle again, but a bit higher, begin climbing the higher ridge east.

1.1   Soft, deep sand.

1.2   At crest, make a tight S-turn and speed through a draw. Great views of Dry Creek Valley.

1.4   Descend curvy sidehill.

1.6   At saddle, take fork left and down.

1.8   Go left and down a rolling rocky trail.

1.9   Cross a new wooden bridge and begin climbing the real hill of this ride. A series of switchbacks and soft spots makes this climb a challenge, so take your time and save your speed for when you need it.

2.1   Steep, bumpy section (3).

2.9   Pass under transmission lines and gain ridgetop. Trail turns to a steepening jeep road as it switches back eastward. Stack Rock is now in your face, but I think it is smiling.

3.3   Another saddle, at 3,550 feet, the summit of this ride. Follow jeep road down and left.

3.6   Bottom out in draw and climb out over a small ridge.

3.9   Descend steeply to Cartwright Road (gravel) via a series of ruts and dips. Caution! Watch out for goathead thorns from this point on. Go right and down Cartwright on marble-sized gravel.

4.6   The second trail on your right will lead back to the same fork that you took up at 1.4 miles.

5.2   Pavement.

5.3   Go right (west) at North Dry Creek Road. Marbles and peas resume. It is mostly level and rolling here.

6.1   Turn left off of North Dry Creek Road and onto a singletrack, back through the meadow and over the bridge to complete the loop.

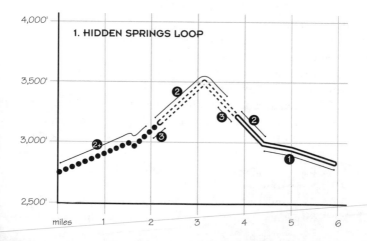

Seamans Gulch–
Dry Creek Loop

Location: West Boise Front, lower foothills.

Distance: 10.6 miles.

Time: 45 to 90 minutes.

Tread: Pavement 8.6 miles; dirt road 2 miles.

Aerobic level: Moderate.

Technical difficulty: 1 to 2.

Hazards: Trucks on first mile of Seamans Gulch Road (headed to landfill); traffic on Highway 55 and Hill Road. The best time to do this loop is during off-peak traffic hours.

Highlights: Gentle grades, fun cruising. This is a good winter ride when the dirt tracks in the foothills are closed.

Land status: Public right-of-way.

Maps: USGS Eagle, Ridge to Rivers Trail System '96, BLM Surface Management Boise '93.

Access: From Boise, take Hill Road west to its intersection with Seamans Gulch, following signs for the landfill. Limited parking is available on a wide shoulder of Seamans Gulch Road; please take care not to block the canal trail that parallels Hill Road.

SEAMANS GULCH— DRY CREEK LOOP
Ride 2

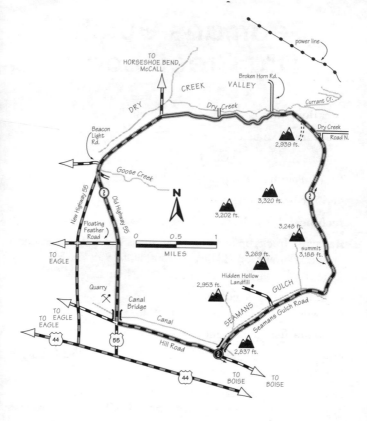

The Ride:

0.0   From the intersection of Hill and Seamans Gulch roads travel northeast (up) Seamans Gulch Road. Watch out for trucks and other traffic headed for the landfill; there is not much of a shoulder on this smooth stretch of pavement. The grade is easy/moderate.

1.1   Stay right where landfill road forks left. The pavement surface degenerates, but so does the traffic. A thick grove of Locust trees borders the gulch on the right.

1.6   Climb out of Seamans Gulch. Grade steepens to higher end of moderate.

2.1   This is the summit of the ride (about 3,200 feet). The patchy blacktop takes some winding turns and affords some great views of Squaw Butte to the northwest. Shift to your big ring.

3.1   Cartwright Road comes in from the right (east). Stay with the main road.

3.3   Roll to the bottom of the hill and start another gentle rise.

3.6   Bear left at fork. To the right is Dry Creek Road North. Stack Rock is visible on the northern skyline. Descend slightly for some nice cruising.

4.0   Pavement turns to dirt here. Stay left at the fork with Broken Horn Road. This section of the road is mostly high-end cruising. A series of 4 small hills requires good momentum in the high ring. The road surface is mostly smooth, well-compacted gravel. Look for pavement here in the near future.

6.0   Join Highway 55 and go left. Exercise caution here as the road joins the highway at a curve. Follow Highway 55 south. This is a 55 mph zone with five lanes and a 10-ft. shoulder. Excercise caution on this section of highway. The grade is flat and wide and, unfortunately, it's great cruising for autos, too.

7.0 Junction with Beacon Light Road. Watch out for traffic. There is a service station here, on the right.

7.1 Cross highway left at big curve. Caution! This is still a high speed section. Cross a six-foot ditch (there are some rock groins you can hop across) and pass through some wood stile posts just left of a curving concrete barrier. This is where the old Highway 55 and the new 55 merge, not for traffic.

7.2 Bear right and up a rising curve of two-lane pavement, following barrier to a moderate grade.

7.5 Top out at hill crest. A view of the Boise Valley opens up. Cruise straight and into the Treasure Valley. Eagle is to your right, and the Owyhee Mountains are straight ahead in the distance.

8.2 Floating Feather Road junction on your right.

9.0 Cross canal bridge. Quarry is to right. Watch for trucks.

9.2 Turn left at Hill Road (flashing yellow light).

10.6 Complete loop at Seamans Gulch. You have now earned your "Road Warrior" badge.

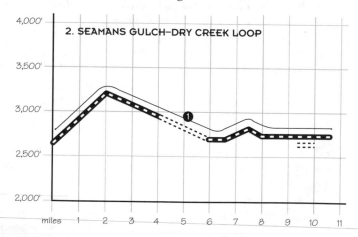

Willow Lane Greenbelt Loop

Location: Boise River West.

Distance: 4.2 miles.

Time: 20 to 25 minutes.

Tread: All paved, dedicated pathway.

Aerobic level: Easy.

Technical difficulty: Easy.

Hazards: Foot and wheeled traffic. A section on the Garden City side, between mile 2.5 and 3.1 is closed between December 15 and February 15 becasue it is wildlife winter habitat area.

Highlights: Almost half of this ride (south of the river, in Garden City) didn't exist until recently; it allows riders and pedestrians to loop the Boise River on both sides. Abundant waterfowl, floaters in the summer, and year-round pathway users can be found here.

Land status: Public.

Maps: Ada County Ridge to Rivers Bikeway, Boise River Greenbelt and Boise City Parks (both in the Boise City Park and Facility Guide), USGS Eagle.

Access: From downtown Boise, go west on State Street for about 4 miles. Turn left onto Willow Lane. Go left at the first paved road into the park complex. Wind around until you reach the main parking lot. The ride starts from middle of the

WILLOW LANE-GREENBELT LOOP
Ride 3

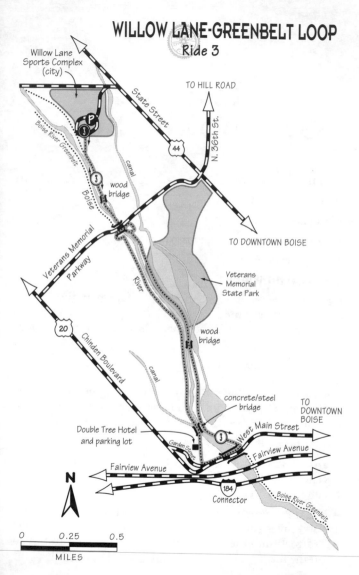

parking area. In summer, there's also drinking water and potties here.

The   Ride:

0.0   From the middle of the main parking area head south
       on pavement towards the Boise River. Watch for autos!
       This can be a busy lot in softball season.

0.1   Go left through stiles onto Boise River Greenbelt
       (BRG).

0.5   Cross long wood plank bridge and estuary so river.

0.6   Pass under Veterans Memorial Parkway Bridge.

0.7   Pathway winds under canopy as you enter Veterans
       Memorial State Park. Note: Taking a left over a wooden
       bridge here will lead you to the main park area, potties,
       and State Street.

0.9   Wind around pond to left (water on both sides now)
       and past site of Old Soldiers Home.

1.4+   Cross wood canal bridge.

1.6   Pass pond on left. Watch for kids and congestion here
       during swim season.

2.0   Go right and off of GRB. Cross Main Street bridge.

2.1   Go right on Garden Street. Watch for traffic! This is one
       of the few short sections where you're exposed to autos.

2.2-   Go right into DoubleTree parking lot. Follow parking
       lot to rear, heading back towards river.

2.2+   Pass through stiles, leaving parking lot, and enter wind-
       ing paved pathway.

2.4-   Stay right where BRG leaves DoubleTree and follows
       river closely.

2.5+   Pass through stiles and cross new canal bridge. **Warn-
       ing:** This is the beginning of a wildlife winter habitat area,
       and the next 0.6 miles of pathway may be closed between

December 15 and February 15. Look for detour information on the gate if the closure is in effect.

3.2+ Pass through a double set of stiles. Watch out for one motorized driveway access on left.

3.4+ Go left up ramp and off BRG. Then go right across Veterans Memorial Parkway bridge. Note: The BRG continues west here under the bridge toward the Ada County Fairgrounds, but as of this writing, is not completed.

3.6 Go right on ramp. Bearing right, pass under bridge, looping back the way we came.

3.7 Cross back over wood brige.

4.1 Go right off BRG.

4.2 Complete ride and loop back at starting point.

Quail–Harrison Hollows Loop

Location: West Boise foothills.

Distance: 4.9 miles.

Time: 25 to 35 minutes.

Tread: Pavement 3.0 miles; doubletrack 1.9 miles.

Aerobic level: Easy.

Technical difficulty: 1 to 3+ on doubletrack.

Hazards: Goathead thorns, chuck holes, hoofprints in some parts of doubletrack; traffic on Hill Road.

Highlights: Easy access, a nice introductory tour of the foothills.

Land status: Public streets, private doubletrack (Please stay on trails!).

Maps: USGS Boise North, Boise city street map.

Access: From downtown Boise, go west on Hill Road to its intersection with 36th Street North. The ride begins here, at Hillside Junior High.

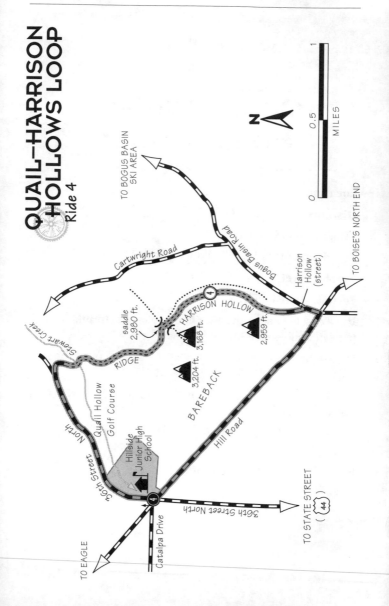

QUAIL–HARRISON HOLLOWS LOOP
Ride 4

The Ride:

0.0 From the corner of Hill Road and 36th Street, go north on 36th, toward the foothills. Pavement rolls and rises.

0.6 Crest out on hill; begin descent past clubhouse and the north end of Quail Hollow Golf Course.

1.1 Turn right on North Eyrie Way. The pavement ends and turns to doubletrack. Caution! There are bad goathead thorns here (on both sides of the creek). It is not a bad idea, especially in summer, to carry your bike.

1.2 Bear left at the second dirt road past the pavement.

1.3 Go right on the first trail, then cross the creek and follow a doubletrack heading east.

1.4 About 50 yards after crossing the creek, go right on a doubletrack that winds left (and up a short steep) onto a low and briskly-rising ridge. Follow ridge.

1.8 Doubletrack leaves ridgetop and snakes around right sidehill.

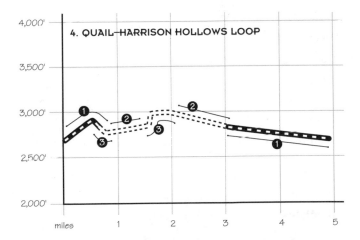

2.0 At 4-way junction in saddle, go straight ahead on the second road from the right (the only one descending) into Harrison Hollow. This is a fast, smooth section of doubletrack with very good visibility, so enjoy it.

3.0 Ride onto Harrison Hollow Street (paved). Follow it to Bogus Basin Road and turn right.

3.3 Turn right at Hill Road. A bike lane on Hill Road makes for some nice cruising, but watch out for those who think that bike lanes are their own personal "parkplatzes." Follow Hill Road back to its intersection with 36th Street to complete the loop.

Stewart Gulch Loop

Location: West Boise foothills.

Distance: 5.9 miles.

Time: 30 to 45 minutes.

Tread: Pavement 4.4 miles; doubletrack 1.2 miles; singletrack 0.3 mile.

Aerobic level: Easy.

Technical difficulty: 1 on pavement; 2 to 3 on doubletrack; 3 on singletrack.

Hazards: Goathead thorns near Stewart Creek; chuck holes; hoofprints; traffic on Hill Road.

Highlights: Easy access and a widely varied ride. Fun and fast.

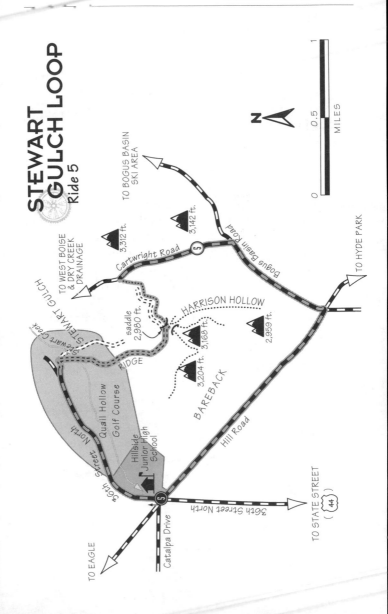

STEWART
GULCH LOOP
Ride 5

N

0   0.5   1
MILES

TO WEST BOISE
& DRY CREEK
DRAINAGE

TO BOGUS BASIN
SKI AREA

Cartwright Road

3,312 ft.

3,142 ft.

Bogus Basin Road

STEWART GULCH

STEWART CREEK

saddle
2,980 ft.

HARRISON HOLLOW

RIDGE

3,168 ft.

2,959 ft.

3,204 ft.

BAREBACK

North Street

36th Street

Quail Hollow
Golf Course

Hillside
Junior High
School

Hill Road

TO HYDE PARK

TO EAGLE

Catalpa Drive

36th Street North

TO STATE STREET
(44)

Land status: Public streets and roads; private single and doubletrack. (Please stay on trails!)

Maps: USGS Boise North, Boise city street map.

Access: From downtown Boise, go west on Hill Road to its intersection with 36th Street North. The ride begins here, at Hillside Junior High.

The Ride:

0.0 From the corner of Hill Road and 36th Street North, go north on 36th towards the foothills. Pavement rolls and rises.

0.7 Crest out on hill; begin descent past clubhouse and the north end of Quail Hollow Golf Course.

1.1 Turn right on North Eyrie Way. The pavement ends and turns to doubletrack.

1.2 Bear left on the second dirt road, past the pavement.

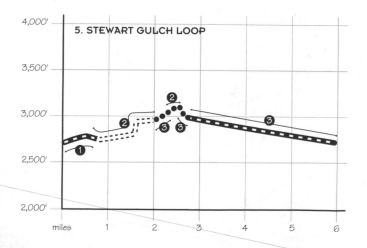

5. STEWART GULCH LOOP

1.3   Go right on the first trail and over the creek. Follow a doubletrack for about 100 yards. Turn right onto another doubletrack.

1.4   Go left on doubletrack up a small ridge, rising steeply at first, then gently.

1.8   Doubletrack leaves ridgetop and snakes around right sidehill.

2.0   At 4-way junction in saddle, go left, up a moderately steep doubletrack.

2.1   A singletrack on your right parallels the doubletrack. Switch to the singletrack and start climbing.

2.2   Return to the doubletrack at a small saddle, then bear left at a small knob. Dip down, then climb a short steep grade.

2.4   Gain saddle. Go left at the singletrack going sidehill and take in the view of downtown Boise, to the right. This section is narrow, brushy, and bumpy (3+).

2.5   Gain ridge. Bear left on doubletrack briefly, then cut across the ridge and dive down to the right on a short steep section (4).

2.6   Go right at Cartwright Road (pavement). Shift into high ring.

2.7   Cruise on a steep, fast downhill.

3.4   Go right at Bogus Basin Road. Smooth and fast.

4.2   Turn right at Hill Road and follow the rolling bike lane back to 36th Street to complete the loop.

Hillside–Harrison Hollow Ridge Loop

Location: Boise Front foothills, just north of Hill Road.

Distance: 5 miles.

Time: 25-45 minutes.

Tread: Doubletrack and singletrack dirt 3.3 miles; pavement 1.7 miles.

Aerobic level: Easy to moderate.

Technical difficulty: Pavement 1; doubletrack 2+, singletrack 4.

Hazards: Steep, narrow sidehill (some exposure), abrupt ramp, traffic on Hill Road.

Highlights: Quick, easy access from town, views, relatively smooth terrain

Land status: Mostly private; please stay on established trails.

Maps: Boise National Forest, USGS Boise North.

Access: In Boise's northwest end, start from Hillside Junior High School at the corner of Hill Road and 36th Street.

The Ride:

0.0 Begin from Hillside Junior High School at the corner of Hill Road and 36th Street. Go to the northeast end of campus, just northeast (uphill) of the tennis courts.

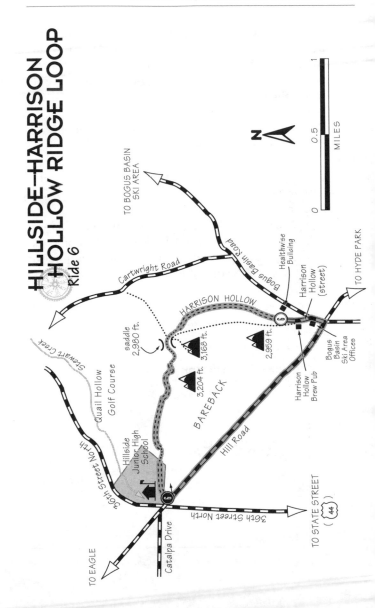

HILLSIDE–HARRISON HOLLOW RIDGE LOOP
Ride 6

N

0   0.5   1

MILES

TO BOGUS BASIN SKI AREA

Cartwright Road

Bogus Basin Road

Healthwise Building

Harrison Hollow (street)

HARRISON HOLLOW

TO HYDE PARK

saddle 2,980 ft.

3,204 ft.

3,168 ft.

2,959 ft.

BAREBACK

Bogus Basin Ski Area Offices

Harrison Hollow Brew Pub

Stewart Creek

Quail Hollow Golf Course

Hillside Junior High School

36th Street North

Hill Road

36th Street North

TO STATE STREET
44

Catalpa Drive

TO EAGLE

0.2 Pedal or push up a wide, steep (!), dirt singletrack that heads directly uphill. (Option: Follow narrow, dirt singletrack that leads gently up to the left; this will swithback at the ridge and meet the more direct route where the ridge levels off.

0.4 Ridge levels off, then dips.

0.7 Trail follows singletrack left (bypass rutted doubletrack to right that heads directly uphill)

0.9 Follow switchback up right to gain ridge.

1.2 Climb to third ridge knoll. Singletrack meets doubletrack here. Zoom left or right of barbed wire fence remains through dip.

1.3 Leave ridge at singletrack left fork. Caution! This section is narrow, and the sidehill is very steep and exposed. Consider walking parts of this section (or outrigging with your uphill leg) if you are feeling less-than-fresh.

1.5 Regain ridge and doubletrack. Very steep, short, downhill section; most will want to walk.

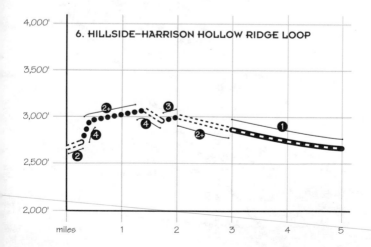

6. HILLSIDE–HARRISON HOLLOW RIDGE LOOP

1.6 Take singletrack left at fork. Rutted doubletrack goes up right. Gentle descent here; trail widens.

1.8 At saddle in Harrison Hollow, take second from left doubletrack (most uphill trail) at 4-way junction. (A smooth, singletrack breaks off right from this doubletrack about 100 feet up from the junction; it parallels and rejoins the doubletrack as you gain the ridgetop.)

2.0 Reach low ridge. Take doubletrack fork to right. Follow east side of Harrison Hollow down on this fun ridge.

2.7 Reach knoll with tacky Christmas star. Stay on ridge. (Note: Due to new development in the lower section of the hollow, coming off the ridge at or near this point will probably be the best route. Look for the new trail, and please be courteous and cautious of the activity in this new neighborhood. This is private land, and it is a privilege to be here.)

3.0 Exercise caution at brief rise in ridge, which drops steeply on the downhill slope bearing right.

3.1 Reach pavement and bottom of Harrison Hollow. (Stopping at the brew pub here is only allowed if you've earned it.)

3.2 Turn right at Bogus Basin Road.

3.3 At Hill Road intersection, turn right, and go 1.7 miles to complete the loop at Highside Junior High.

Boise Greenbelt–
Oregon Trail Loop

Location: Boise River from downtown southeast, out past Lucky Peak Dam and back on the south side of the river along the Oregon Trail.

Distance: 27.1 miles.

Time: 3 to 4 hours.

Tread: 17.7 miles on pavement (mostly greenbelt pathway); 8.3 miles on doubletrack/dirt road (mostly Old Oregon Trail); 1.1 miles on singletrack.

Aerobic level: Moderate to strenuous.

Technical difficulty: 1 on pavement; 2 to 3 on doubletrack; 2 to 4 on singletrack.

Hazards: Traffic on greenbelt; rocks, dust, or mud on/off pavement.

Highlights: This long loop takes you from the heart of the city to a very remote section of trail. Lucky Peak Dam and Reservoir at Barclay Bay, Discovery State Park, Sandy Point Beach, and Barber Park, all part of the Boise River system, are just a few of the major attractions on this ride. The southern rim of the Boise River Canyon has many hidden, shady spots, along the more urban parts of the river, that are waiting to be discovered. This ride is mostly flat and paved, but the middle section along the Oregon Trail and the climb out of Sandy Point offer a challenge.

Land status: Mostly public (city, county, state, BLM), with a private section along the Oregon Trail. Please be aware that public access through this private section ia a privilege that can be revoked at any time.

Maps: Boise River Greenbelt and City Parks Map (in the Boise City Park and Facility Guide), Ada County Ridge to Rivers Bikeway; USGS Boise South and Lucky Peak.

Access: Go to Ann Morrison Park, just west of downtown Boise on the river's south bank. The main auto access is from Americana Avenue. The ride starts here.

The Ride:

0.0   Start ride at playground/restroom facilities at Ann Morrison Park. These are located close to the Boise River. Ample parking is available nearby at either of two parking lots. Pedal southeast (upstream) on the greenbelt pathway that follows the river's south bank.

0.1   Go left, and cross the river over an arch pathway bridge. Turn right after the bridge and follow the paved pathway upstream on the north side of river.

0.6   Pass through two tunnels and come out behind the city library. Pass through wooden post stiles and cross under Capitol Boulevard.

0.7   Go right (toward river) on then greenbelt pathway, which is defined by a concrete barrier.

1.0   Stay left as the pathway forks. The right fork leads to Boise State University, across the river.

1.6   Pass under Broadway.

2.2   Morrison Knudsen Nature Center is on your left.

2.3   Boise Tourist Park (Municipal Park), on your left, is one of Boise's oldest.

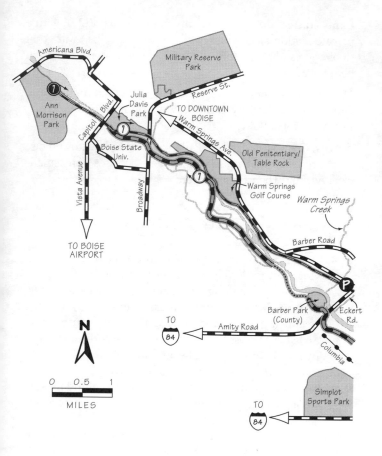

BOISE GREENBELT–OREGON TRAIL LOOP
Ride 7

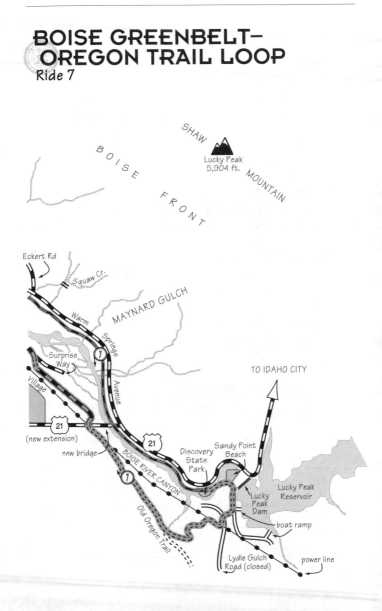

SHAW MOUNTAIN

Lucky Peak
5,904 ft.

BOISE FRONT

Eckert Rd

Squaw Cr.

MAYNARD GULCH

Warm Springs Avenue

Surprise Way

Village

21
(new extension)

new bridge

BOISE RIVER CANYON

Old Oregon Trail

TO IDAHO CITY

Discovery State Park

Sandy Point Beach

Lucky Peak Dam

boat ramp

Lucky Peak Reservoir

Lydle Gulch Road (closed)

power line

2.4 Bear right at Y in pathway. Now, you are leaving the shaded canopy of trees in the downtown area. So if it is summer, better butter up here.

2.7 Go right at pathway fork. The left fork leads to the Natatorium and Warm Springs Avenue.

5.8 You are out in the flat of the prairie now. The Kelly Hot Springs historical sign is here.

6.4 Cross Eckert Road. Caution! This is a choke point, and traffic can back up here.

7.5 Swoop down and to the right, away from the main roadway. Glide a rare bit (no cheese).

9.0 Pass under the Highway 21 bridge.

9.3 Go up a short hill and past Diversion Dam, which is on your right.

11.0 Enter Discovery State Park. There are water and restroom facilities here; also shade and historical signs. Stay on paved pathway.

11.3 Bear right as the pathway splits to follow the river. Lucky Peak Dam and Spillway are visible upstream.

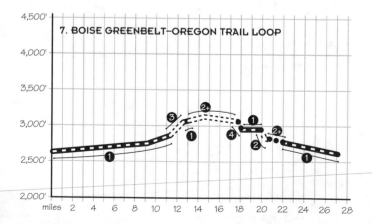

11.6 At Lucky Peak State Park(Sandy Point Beach pathway entry) go right on paved road.

11.7 Just left of the power plant front gate is a gravel service road. The road bars motorized travel with a metal gate and sign. Pass around the gate and pedal up the road. It is relatively steep with a soft gravel surface.

12.0 Bear left at Y. Continue up an easier grade.

12.1 Grade steepens.

12.4 Pass through a steel gate and enter Lucky Peak Reservoir parking lot and boat ramp. Stay to right on main paved road. To see the water itself, just go to the far side of the lot, on the left.

12.6 Turn right, off of the pavement, onto a dirt road that splits immediately. Take the right fork of the dirt road, which is bumpy and rutted, but relatively flat.

12.7 Bear left at Y onto a rutted doubletrack. (Right goes downhill to Foote Park.)

12.8 Turn off of this road and onto a dirt doubletrack that drops to the right. A railroad-tie fencepost is the only distinguishing feature here. The track is rutted and rocky.

13.0 From the bottom of the gulch, begin climbing moderate hill. Difficulty hovers around 3 from here to pavement (the next 5 miles).

13.4 Go through chained but not locked gate. Please close it; you are on private range land now. Grade flattens. Doubletrack continues with a loose, rocky surface: golfballs to cantaloupes.

13.9 Cross gulch bottom; grade steepens to moderate. Surface mellows.

14.5 Merge with road coming in from the left. This is the Old Oregon Trail proper. Bear right on rutted dirt. When wet, this is soup; when dry, this is powder.

15.6 Pass through closed barbed wire gate, making sure to close it. Go right on gravel road.

16.1 Junction of gravel and paved county roads. Take an immediate right, off of the pavement and onto a dirt doubletrack.

16.4 Cross under power lines.

16.5 Stay to the south side of the Boise River Canyon rim.

16.6 View of Canyon mouth and Highway 21 bridge.

16.8 Take middle trail at a three-way fork. This winds around through some rocky terrain.

17.8 Go right at fork. This leads down off the rim, and is somewhat steep and rocky, so use caution. Cross under two big transmission lines.

18.0 At Highway 21, go right down a gentle grade.

18.3 Turn left, off Highway 21, just opposite the Oregon Trail Interpretive Center, which is on the right. Bear right just after leaving the highway, following the eastern edge of the rimrock. (Option: Rather than turning left here and following the top of the rim for the next mile, you can continue down the highway grade to the bottom of the upper rimrock slope. Then take the first trail left off of Highway 21; this will lead to a path that hugs the rimrock bottom, via Surprise Valley, which will bring you to Surprise Way and eventually to Amity/Eckert Roads and Barber Park. It is an equally long, somewhat easier route.)

18.5 Cross under transmission lines and then bear left on a dirt doubletrack. This is the Oregon Trail again. The trail continues along the top of the rimrock, beneath the power lines.

19.7 Drop off of the rimtop and down a singletrack to the right. You should be just above a large water tank at the rim's bottom. The singletrack (3+) is steep, and slick when wet.

19.8 Go left on a gravel access road and pass the water tank (on your left). The grade eases off slightly. At the bend in the road, check out the basalt rock wall remnants of some pioneer structure (on your left).

20.1 Turn left at the paved pathway on the far (north) side of Surprise Way. Follow the pathway west.

20.3 Go right at Amity Road, which soon turns into Eckert Road. This section is a large S-turn that descends moderately and crosses the Boise River Canal. Exercise caution here! This piece of roadway is heavily travelled, especially in summer.

20.6 Turn left at Barber Park (Ada County). Travel on the main park road and keep bearing left until you reach the far end of the park. (An alternative to going through Barber Park proper is to bear left of the entry shack on a paved 1-lane road; this takes you briefly against motorized traffic, but eases you around the crowds and confusion on a big float day).

20.9 Go right when you come to the greenbelt pathway.

21.0 Go right at Y in pathway.

21.1 Pathway turns to dirt singletrack. Caution! In spring, high water can come up over the trail along this section.

22.0 Go left at pedestrian/bike separation. This is the start of a detour around a sensitive wetland area on the river. Route follows Parkcenter Boulevard.

22.9 Go right at River Run. The pathway gives way to a bike lane on the street.

23.7 Turn right at Riverstone.

23.8 Go right onto greenbelt again, following the river closely.

25.3 Cross wooden bridge, bearing right.

25.5 Pass under Broadway and enter Boise State University campus. The pathway along here blends somewhat with the roadway. Just stay close to the river and be ready for dense foot and bike traffic.

26.4 Cross under Capitol Boulevard and over a unique radial wooden bridge. When the water is high, it surges up on both sides of this structure. Re-enter Ann Morrison Park, and complete loop at starting point. Congratulate yourself by drinking at least as much water as whatever else you choose. The history quiz on the Oregon Trail will be postponed until your next reincarnation.

Cartwright–Pierce Park Loop

Location: Foothills of northwest Boise.

Distance: 11.5 miles.

Time: 45 to 60 minutes.

Tread: Pavement 9.3 miles; gravel road 2.2 miles.

Aerobic level: Moderate.

Technical difficulty: 1 on pavement; 2 on gravel.

Hazards: Traffic on Hill Road; soft and rocky spots on gravel; sand on pavement.

Highlights: A good winter ride, easy access, and easy cruising with only one big hill.

Land status: Public roads.

Maps: USGS Boise North and Eagle.

CARTWRIGHT—PIERCE PARK LOOP
Ride 8

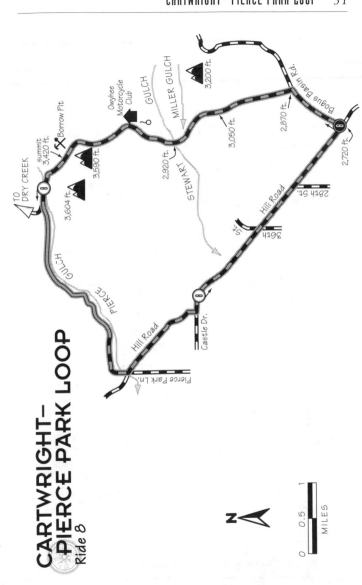

TO DRY CREEK

summit 3,420 ft.

Borrow Pit

Owhee Motorcycle Club

GULCH

MILLER GULCH

3,200 ft.

2,870 ft.

3,050 ft.

2,920 ft.

3,590 ft.

3,604 ft.

STEWART

Bogus Basin Rd.

2,720 ft.

28th St.

36th St.

36th St.

Hill Road

PIERCE GULCH

Hill Road

Castle Dr.

Pierce Park Ln.

N

0   0.5   1
MILES

Access: From Boise, drive to the intersection of Hill and Bogus Basin roads. The ride starts here. Parking is usually available in the Bogus Basin Ski Area parking lot (just South of Shaver's supermarket) during the off season for skiers.

The Ride:

0.0 Go north on Bogus Basin Road to Cartwright Road. A large chuch is on the left side of Cartwright.

0.6 Turn left (west) at Cartwright Road. Gentle grade eases, then continues.

2.0 Climb steadily to hilltop, before dropping into Stewart Gulch. The gulch resembles a little hidden valley from this vantage; and Boise seems far away from this pastoral scene. Do not get cocky, though; this was not the real hill. Shift into your big ring; you will want all the momentum you can get for a good start at the summit.

3.0 After a zoomer, begin climbing out of Stewart Gulch through a series of dips and bends. The grade steepens steadily toward the summit. Watch for sand on the pavement.

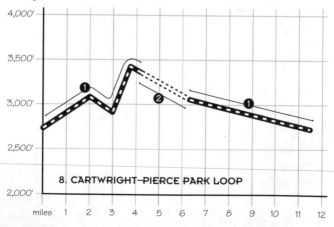

8. CARTWRIGHT–PIERCE PARK LOOP

3.6 Top out at crest. Good views up Dry Creek Valley.

4.0 Bear left at a fork to enter Pierce Gulch. The right fork takes Cartwright Road into the Dry Creek drainage. Here, the surface turns to gravel . Watch out for soft spots, loose gravel, rocky sections, and oblivious motorists.

6.2 Pavement resumes and straightens out; gulch opens up.

6.8 Turn left at junction with Hill Road.

8.1 Come to tee and stop sign; this is where Hill Road meets Castle (to the right). To stay on Hill Road, go left at this tee. Hill Road has mostly wide shoulders (with bike lanes in most places), but some mistake these for parking lanes. Also, use caution when approaching the junctions of Collister, 36th Street, and 28th Street, especially during rush hours. Follow Hill Road to its intersection with Bogus Basin Road to complete the loop.

Cartwright–Dry Creek Loop

Location: Foothills, northwest of Boise.

Distance: 17.4 miles.

Time: 1.5 to 2 hours.

Tread: 15.6 miles on pavement; 1.8 miles on gravel road.

Aerobic level: Moderate to strenuous.

CARTWRIGHT—DRY CREEK LOOP
Ride 9

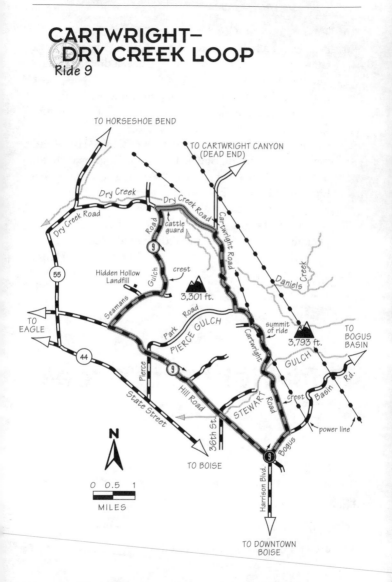

TO HORSESHOE BEND

TO CARTWRIGHT CANYON
(DEAD END)

Dry Creek

Dry Creek Road

Dry Creek Road

Cartwright Road

cattle guard

9

crest

Hidden Hollow Landfill

Seamans Gulch Road

3,301 ft.

Daniels Creek

Park Road

PIERCE GULCH

Cartwright

summit of ride

3,793 ft.

TO BOGUS BASIN

55

TO EAGLE

44

Pierce

9

GULCH

Hill Road

36th St.

STEWART Road

crest

Basin Rd.

power line

State Street

9

Bogus

Harrison Blvd.

TO BOISE

TO DOWNTOWN BOISE

N

0   0.5   1
MILES

Technical difficulty: 1 on pavement; 2 on gravel.

Hazards: Watch out for type-As driving their shiny Suburbans (and other upwardly mobile rigs) and chatting on their cell phones, these people are generally not bike riders themselves. The gravel section of this ride consists of material mostly between the size of peas and marbles; consider them neolithic ball bearings. A fast approaching cloud of dust, while being an immediate hazard, has the ambiguous benefit of warning you early of the cell-heads.

Highlights: The middle reaches of the Dry Creek drainages, paradoxically, are sub-irrigated, and provide welcome verdure, even through midsummer. Traffic is generally very light, and the roads are well maintained. A couple of serious hills are enough to make you appreciate the flats. Although you begin and end in the city, this ride is rural.

Land status: Public roads.

Maps: USGS Boise North, Eagle; Boise National Forest, BLM Boise Front.

Access: From downtown Boise, go to the intersection of Hill and Bogus Basin roads in the north end. The ride starts here.

The Ride:

0.0 From the intersection of Hill and Bogus Basin roads, ride up (north) Bogus Basin Road. It is a smooth, gentle to moderate grade.

0.8 Turn left at Cartwright Road, a gentle grade.

1.2 Pavement narrows.

1.4 Grade increases to moderate.

1.6 Begin downhill to Stewart Gulch.

2.3 Pedal through the gulch.

2.8   Crest a small hill as the grade levels out and the road takes a series of turns.

3.0   Owyhee Motorcycle Club Road is on your right. Stay left, on the main road. The grade becomes steep as you begin this ride's big climb.

3.6   Grade eases.

3.9   The summit. Cruise down; shift to big ring.

4.4   Go right at Cartwright Road fork. To the left is Pierce Park Road. Begin slight uphill.

4.7   Crest. Cruise down. You're now in the Dry Creek drainage.

5.9   Cross creek bottom. Begin gentle climb.

6.4   Crest the hill and go over a cattleguard. Then go left on a gravel road (North Dry Creek Road). Cartwright Road goes up to the right here; it is a dead end to through traffic.

6.6   Gravel road descends moderately. Watch those peas and marbles!

7.6   Cross creek bottom, onto flat trail.

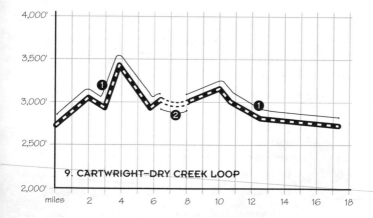

9. CARTWRIGHT–DRY CREEK LOOP

8.1 Climb a small hill.

8.2 Pavement resumes.

8.3 Go left at main Dry Creek Road.

8.4 Pedal up moderate grade. This is the second main hill of this ride.

9.6 Steep grade.

9.8 Crest hill and descend into Seamans Gulch. Shift to your big ring.

10.8 Hidden Hollow Landfill Road to right. Stay left on main road and watch out for traffic!

12.0 Turn left at Hill Road. There are bike lanes on most of Hill Road, but be aware; some people use them for parking RVs, horse trailers, etc.

14.4 Go left where Hill Road meets Castle Road; this will keep you on Hill.

17.4 Complete loop where Hill Road meets Bogus Basin Road.

Crane Creek–Corrals Loop

Location: Immediate Boise Front foothills; close to town. Follows Crane Creek drainage and west to descend Bogus Basin Road.

Distance: 9.8 miles.

Time: 1.5 hours.

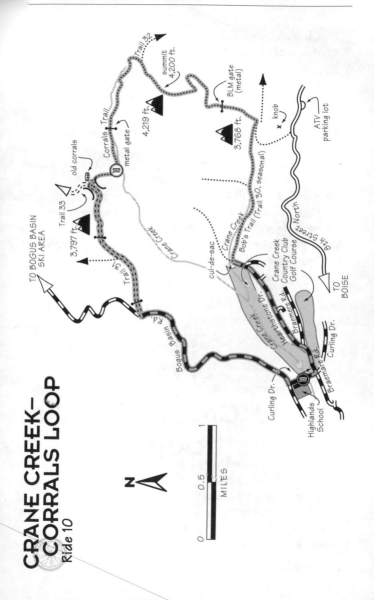

CRANE CREEK–CORRALS LOOP
Ride 10

N

MILES
0   0.5   1

TO BOGUS BASIN SKI AREA

Trail 32
summit 4,200 ft.
Corrals Trail
4,219 ft.
BLM gate (metal)
3,768 ft.
metal gate
old corrals
Trail 33
3,797 ft.
Trail 31
Crane Creek
knob
x
ATV parking lot
Crane Creek
Bob's Trail (Trail 30, seasonal)
cul-de-sac
Crane Creek Country Club Golf Course
9th Street North
TO BOISE
Bogus Basin Rd.
Crane Creek Dr.
Hearthstone Dr.
Braemere Rd.
Braemere Rd.
Curling Dr.
Curling Dr.
Highlands School

Tread: 3.4 miles pavement; 1.6 miles dirt/rock/sand 2-track, 4.8 miles singletrack.

Aerobic level: intermediate/advanced.

Technical difficulty: 2-3 on doubletrack, 2-5 on singletrack.

Hazards: Big boulders, narrow sidehill track in Crane Creek bottom, sand pockets. Patchy pavement and traffic on Bogus Basin Road.

Highlights: Big boulders, stream crossings, narrow sidehill track in Crane Creek bottom, sand pockets. Traffic on Bogus Basin Road.

Land status: Private, BLM, and state land.

Maps: Boise National Forest; USGS Boise North, Ridge to Rivers.

Access: A little more than a mile north of the Bogus Basin Road and Hill Road intersection, park at Highlands Elementary School, on the right at the corner of Curling Drive. There is usually an empty parking lot after hours and on weekends, but if it looks like there's any crunch, park away from the school. The ride starts from the school parking lot.

The   Ride:

- 0.0 Head southeast (right from the lot) up Curling Drive. Pavement is smooth.
- 0.2 Turn left onto Braemere Road. Hill becomes steep, cuts through Crane Creek Golf Course.
- 0.5 Turn left onto Hearthstone Drive. Street dips slightly and then climbs consistently.
- 1.3 Bear left at junction with Harcourt.
- 1.5 Take singletrack on right (north) side at the end of the cul de sac. It's an obvious trail that leads up the rocky creek bottom. This is Trail 30 (Bob's Trail); the next 1.5

miles is highly technical: stream crossings, boulders and thin sidehill ahead.

1.8   Pass concrete sediment dam and pump up short, rutted steep.

1.9   Top out over earth dam and dip down left.

2.0   Stay to main trail on right. Grade eases, takes sidehill.

2.3   Cross Crane Creek again.

2.4 to 2.8 Numerous crossings of Crane Creek, rocky (4+) obstacles.

2.9   Go through single bar gate.

3.0   Short steep burst. Punch it!

3.1   Trail 30 marker (faces uphill) and fork. Take wide dirt singletrack left, Trail number 1, up gentle and smooth. (right fork takes you to 8th street)

3.5   Junction of Trails 31 and 1 (Trail 1 ends here.) Follow Trail 31 to left.

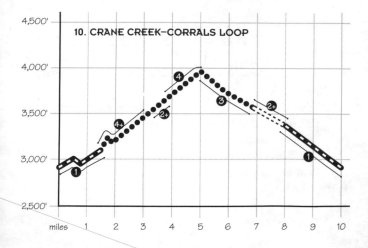

3.6 Go through metal gate (leaving BLM land). Climb moderately.

4.0 Gain rise, then descend briefly.

4.2 Climb out of dip and over wood bridge.

4.8 Reach top of ridge, top of ride. Cruise ruts and rollers.

5.0 Bear left and down. Trail 32 heads up right here.

6.1 Metal gate. Trail flattens and rolls, then climb briefly.

6.4 Track widens to doubletrack now.

6.5 Pass old corrals on right, stay left. Trail 33 goes right, past corrals.

7.0 Pass through metal gate and fence.

7.2 Singletrack goes right to new Corrals trailhead on Bogus Basin Road.

8.0 Go through gate at junction with Bogus Basin Road. Go left (down) Bogus Basin Road. Watch out for traffic.

9.8 There is a 3-way stop at the corner of Curling Drive and Bogus Basin Road. Drift in to the Highlands School parking lot, wearing your mud in style.

Corrals—8th Street Loop

Location: Boise foothills, just northwest of the center of town.

Distance: 12 miles.

Time: 1.5 to 2.5 hours.

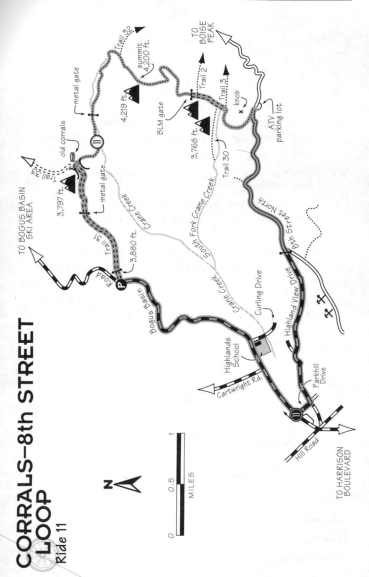

CORRALS–8th STREET LOOP
Ride 11

N

MILES
0   0.5   1

TO HARRISON BOULEVARD

Hill Road

Parkhill Drive

Cartwright Rd.

Highlands School

Highland View Drive

8th Street North

Curling Drive

Crane Creek

South Fork Crane Creek

Trail 30

Trail 3, knob

ATV parking lot

Trail 2

TO BOISE PEAK

BLM gate

3,768 ft.

4,219 ft.

summit 4,200 ft.

Trail 32

metal gate

old corrals

Trail 33

3,797 ft.

metal gate

Trail 31

3,880 ft.

Bogus Basin Road

TO BOGUS BASIN SKI AREA

Tread. 5.3 miles on pavement (start and finish); 1.7 miles of doubletrack; 5 miles of singletrack.

Aerobic level: Moderate with several short, steep sections.

Technical difficulty: 1 on pavement; 2 to 3 on doubletrack; 3 to 4+ on singletrack.

Hazards: Traffic on Bogus Basin Road; narrow shoulders in places, traffic (both autos and bikes) on the descent down 8th Street. Doubletrack has sand pockets; singletrack has sharp, rocky sections.

Highlights: Quick, easy access from town, varied terrain with a mixture of skill levels. Better-than-postcard views of Boise and the surrounding Front Range.

Land status: About half of this ride is on private land; stay on marked trails only. The remainder is BLM and state land. Please obey the side trail closure signs; they're there to protect habitat.

Maps: Boise National Forest, USGS Boise North, Ridge to Rivers.

Access: In Boise's north end go 1/3 mile north on Bogus Basin Road from its intersection with Hill Road to Parkhill Drive. The ride starts at the corner of Parkhill Drive and Bogus Basin Road. Parking is available on Parkhill Drive.

The Ride:

0.0   Pedal north up Bogus Basin Road 2.5 miles to wire gate on the right. Beware of traffic, narrow shoulders in places, and a less-than-perfect paved surface. Grade is moderate, but sustained.

2.5   Turn off Bogus Basin Road through a barbed wire gate visible on right (east) side. Note wide turnout on opposite side of road; it provides limited parking. Follow soft doubletrack through gate. Trail hugs gently inclined ridge.

3.5   Go through metal gate. Nice views; ridge tops out.

3.9   Pass old corrals and trail fork on left. Trail to left leads up to the higher reaches of the Boise Front. Follow main doubletrack right, through draw.

4.2   Trail turns to soft singletrack. Descend Crane Creek gully, which narrows and steepens. Good turns here; do not miss the interesting granite outcroppings.

4.4   Go through metal gate at creek bottom.

4.7   Trail ascends and grade steepens; watch for ruts.

5.4   Stay on main trail, which switchbacks to right (a singletrack goes left here), and traverse ridge.

5.6   Gain ridge and climb.

5.7   Reach summit of ride and full view. Deteriorating doubletrack heads down relatively steep, rocky, and rutted hill.

6.3   Cross Crane Gulch. Climb.

6.4   Take right fork down to another draw.

6.9   Go through metal gate; enter BLM land. Stay on main dirt doubletrack. Go through draw and climb.

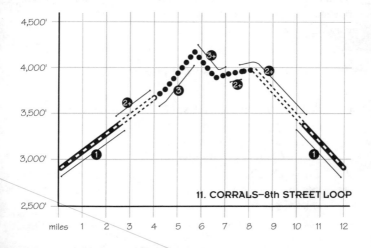

11. CORRALS–8th STREET LOOP

7.4 Reach saddle and trail tee. Bear right; follow dirt singletrack on sidehill grade.

8.2 At 8th Street (a wide, primitive road) turn right (west) and head down toward town. Beware of horses, pedestrians, hot rods, and dirt bikes. ATV parking lot is just across road.

10.2 Exit 8th Street on right over dirt berm onto Highland View Drive (pavement). Descend through winding residential neighborhood. Caution! Driveways.

11.8 Turn right on Parkhill Drive. Go the 2 blocks which return you to Bogus Basin Road and the completion of this loop.

Hulls Gulch—Crane Creek Loop

Location: Lower foothills, north of downtown Boise.

Distance: 9.2 miles.

Time: 90 to 120 minutes.

Tread: 2.8 miles on pavement; 1.1 miles on doubletrack/dirt road; 5.3 miles on singletrack.

Aerobic level: Moderate to strenuous.

Technical difficulty: 1 on pavement; 2 to 4 on doubletrack; 3 to 5 on singletrack.

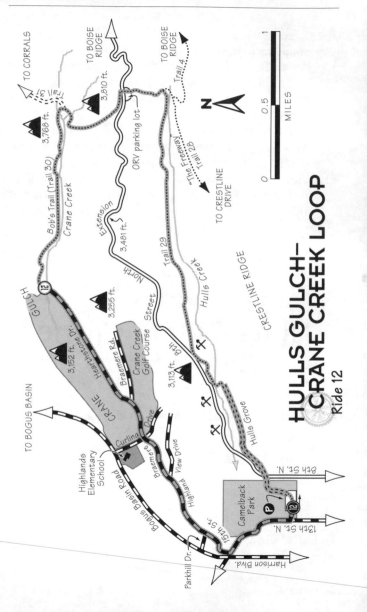

**HULLS GULCH–
CRANE CREEK LOOP**
Ride 12

Hazards: Traffic (on trail and off), humps, ruts, rocks, steeps, sand, poison ivy, you name it! Adding to the natural difficulty of the topography is the likelihood that you will meet some fool doing the same thing you are, but in the opposite direction. If you are lucky, it will not happen on one of the many blind spots. Watch for new flood mitigation structures and detours in lower Bob's Trail.

Highlights: This is a tour-de-force of the lower foothills. This loop contains some of the most sustained singletrack you'll find in this area. To be able to ride the difficult lower Hulls and Crane gulches is something to work at.

Land status: City, state, BLM, and some private.

Maps: USGS Boise North, BLM Boise Front, Ridge to Rivers Trail System

Access: From downtown Boise go north on 13th Street to Camel Back Park . The ride starts from the parking lot by the tennis courts.

The Ride:

0.0   From the parking lot just west of the tennis courts at Camel Back Park pedal east around the courts until you gain a singletrack cutting across the lawn, heading toward the base of the hill. Gain a dirt singletrack and follow.

0.3   At small rise go through a steel gate.

0.4   Bear right and cross creek, then make a left onto a dirt doubletrack.

0.6   Cross pavement (8th Street), continue on doubletrack, and go through steel gate.

1.0   This is lower Hulls Grove; it is mostly shaded and very well used. Bear left at doubletrack (top of Hulls Grove loop) and then go right at doubletrack, which turns to singletrack, heading toward creek.

1.1   Drop into creek bottom and cross, then climb out. Go right at 8th Street (gravel road).

1.2   Turn off road onto singletrack to the right. This is a wonderful warm-up for what is yet to come.

1.5   At fork go either way. The trails meet again to the west of the creek bottom.

1.7   Start climb up soft and sandy section. Keep your eyes up! The presence of other people here is more hazardous than the trail itself.

1.9   Difficulty 4. Steep short climb and dips. Cross creek.

2.2   Short, steep sections.

2.3   Mini-crest. From this point on, technical difficulty is a sustained 4+ for the rest of Hulls Gulch.

3.0   Enter public lands. Up through obstacle (difficulty 5), over World Class Obstacle (WCO, difficulty 5+). Poison ivy, too!

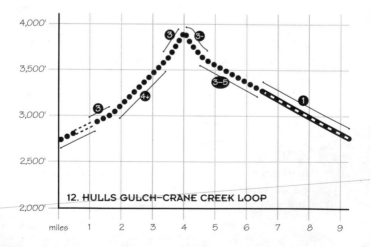

12. HULLS GULCH–CRANE CREEK LOOP

3.5 Go up and left at trail junction. Climb moderate to steep switchbacks.

4.0 Gain pines and all-terrain vehicle parking area. Follow level doubletrack that heads toward upper 8th Street. There are restroom facilities here. Cross road and head left on singletrack, along fenceline marked with Trail 1 sign. Summit of ride at 3,800 feet.

4.7 Reach saddle and fork. Go left and down initially steep, narrow singletrack. This is Trail 30 (Bob's Trail). Caution! Technical difficulty for the bulk of remaining singletrack is 4+, with numerous 5 places. Watch for detours and recent trail work.

5.0 Go over bar gate, then rocky and narrow 5.

5.1 WCO, 5 +.

5.3 Difficulty 5, rocks.

5.4 Difficulty 5, poison ivy.

5.6 Trail, terrain opens up somewhat. Grade flattens and rises gently.

5.9 Difficulty 5, then down short steep section to boulders and sand in gulch bottom.

6.0 Difficulty 5, creek bottom boulders.

6.4 Come to paved cul-de-sac. Bear left and up hill, then right on Hearthstone Drive.

7.3 Climb short hill.

7.4 Crest and right at Braemere Road, then cruise down steep hill.

7.7 Cross Curling Drive and go up hill. Stay on Braemere.

8.0 Go right on Highlands Avenue. Cruise curves.

8.7 Turn left on Hill Road. Follow back to Camelback Park and complete loop.

Lucky Peak Loop

Location: Boise Front, northwest of downtown Boise.

Distance: 25.3 miles.

Time: 3 to 5 hours.

Tread: 10.6 miles of pavement (road and greenbelt); 13.3 miles of doubletrack/dirt road; 1.4 miles of singletrack.

Aerobic level: Strenuous.

Technical difficulty: 1 to 2 on pavement; 1 to 3+ on doubletrack; 2 to 3+ on singletrack.

Hazards: Bogus Basin Road has rough patchwork sections and sand (over pavement) in spots. Doubletrack has sand pockets, ruts, loose rock; singletrack has narrow, exposed, and rocky sections with narrow openings in summer. Trail 11 (West Highland Valley Trail) is closed January 1 through April 1 for wintering deer and elk.

Highlights: This is a big loop. Terrain is varied while rough and rocky surfaces are limited to short sections. Steep climbs are sustained, but only severe for short sections. The canopy of conifers is not nearly as full as the more northern sections of the Boise Ridge; you are in the sun more and exposed to the elements. Finishing with the greenbelt and Warm Springs Avenue, you feel quite urbane after descending from the eagles.

Land status: Some of this ride is on private land; stay on marked trails only. The remainder is BLM and state land and national forest land. Please obey the side trail closure signs; they're there to protect habitat.

LUCKY PEAK LOOP
Ride 13

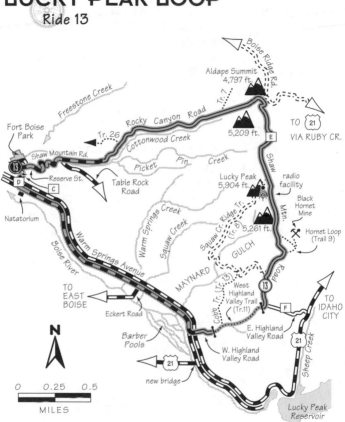

Boise Ridge Rd.

Aldape Summit
4,797 ft.

Tr. 7

Freestone Creek

Rocky Canyon Road

Tr. 26

Cottonwood Creek

5,209 ft.

E

TO 21
VIA RUBY CR.

Fort Boise
Park

Shaw Mountain Rd.

13

Reserve St.

Picket   Pin   Creek

D

C

Table Rock
Road

Lucky Peak
5,904 ft.

radio
facility

Shaw Mtn. Road

Black
Hornet
Mine

Natatorium

Warm Springs Creek

Squaw Creek

Squaw Cr. Ridge Tr.

Tr. 8   5,261 ft.

Hornet Loop
(Trail 9)

Boise River

Warm Springs Avenue

MAYNARD   GULCH

13

West
Highland
Valley Trail
(Tr.11)

Cobb Tr. (Tr. 13)

TO
EAST
BOISE

Eckert Road

F

TO
IDAHO
CITY

Barber
Pools

E. Highland
Valley Road

21

W. Highland
Valley Road

Sheep Creek

N

0   0.25   0.5

21

new bridge

MILES

Lucky Peak
Reservoir

Shafer Butte, BLM Boise Front, Ridge to Rivers.

Access: From downtown Boise go north to Fort Street and Garrison Road (an entrance to Fort Boise Park). Drive up Garrison to just across from the tennis courts on left. Bathrooms and ballparks are on the right. Ample parking (except during ball games) is all around. The ride starts here.

The Ride:

0.0   From the corner of Garrison Road and Collins in the Fort Boise Park (just across from the tennis courts) follow Garrison Road north and bear right around the ball fields on some patchy gravel (Scout Lane). Bear left and follow short singletrack which leads through to Reserve Street.

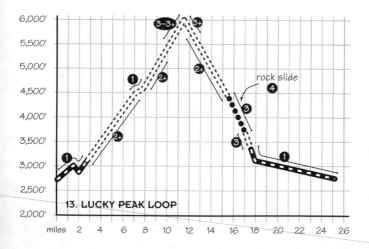

13. LUCKY PEAK LOOP

0.2 Bear left, crossing canal, and up Reserve Street.

0.4 Go right at the end of Reserve up Shaw Mountain Road. Pavement climbs briskly.

1.5 Bear left up Rocky Canyon Road (where Table Rock Road splits from Shaw Mountain Road). This is a small crest, so there's a nice, easy, gliding cruise.

1.9 Cross cattle guards and dip as you cross Cottonwood Creek. Caution.

2.0 Begin winding and rolling climb.

2.8 Pavement ends. Road bears left up steeper grade.

3.1 This is the mouth of the canyon. Large rock crags tower over the road. Some of the rocks are climbing quality, with the most striking formations jutting directly over Cottonwood Creek.

4.0 Pass under a creek-bottom grove of cottonwood, willow, and locust. The shade is welcome even in the spring.

4.6 Come to public lands (BLM) marker. Grade steepens.

5.4 Pass steel gate and cable on left. Fivemile Creek joins the canyon here.

6.3 Just before a 20-foot-high granite hoodoo, a doubletrack heads off to the left; pass on by.

6.7 Doubletrack goes left with gate and marker. This is Orchard Gulch.

7.3 Doubletrack goes right, crosses Cottonwood Creek and leads into fir trees. This road connects with Shaw Mountain Road and leads over into Deer Creek drainage above Lucky Peak Reservoir.

7.8 This is the junction of Rocky Canyon and Shaw Mountain Roads. Go right on Shaw Mountain Road, which is also called Trail E. It is less demanding than Rocky Canyon Road in both grade and surface. Inclines are gentler, and smooth, compacted sand and dirt prevail.

9.8 At a 4-way fork bear right (up) and stay on Trail E.

Reach a small crest and glide down.

10.0 Pump up a steep, rutted hill. Difficulty goes to 3+.

10.1 Bear right at fork up steep, rutted, and rocky hill.

10.6 Steep climb, then soft and sandy trail.

10.7 Bear right up main trail; becomes steep.

10.8 Crest to dip and glide and then a series of dips and glides.

11.2 Steep climb. Then pass Trail 8 marker and junction on right. Continue heading straight on Trail E.

11.3 Come to cattleguard. Difficulty goes to 3+. Ascend rocky and steep hill.

11.5 Reach crest and summit of this ride. (If you go right, off the main trail, at the next fork, you will come to the true top of Lucky Peak. Elevation 5,902 feet.)

11.6 Go left at fork. This takes you around the north side of Lucky Peak itself. Begin smooth, cruising descent.

11.8 Cross cattleguard, fenceline. Views of Boise River Valley and Lucky Peak Reservoir.

12.3 Descent steepens. Difficulty goes to 3+; soft and rocky spots.

12.9 Zoom through dip and climb to crest.

13.2 Cross cattleguard. Trail 9 is to left; stay right on Trail E.

14.0 Another cattleguard.

14.6 Bottom of Trail 8 is to right; stay left and down on Trail E.

15.5 Go right and up dirt road marked Trail 11.

15.7 Go through boom gate, bearing right down Trail 11. This is the old Highland Valley Road. Doubletrack degenerates to a rocky, rutted, and sometimes exposed singletrack. Difficulty goes to 3+.

16.8 Rock slide area. Caution!

17.0 Trail 13 is to right. Stay left and down.

17.3 Pass through boom gate (bottom of Trail 11) and onto gravel road.

17.5 Come onto pavement of Highland Valley Road. Shift into high ring.

17.8 Turn left at Warm Springs Avenue, cross and then take an immediate right down a doubletrack. Watch for ruts in short steep section.

17.9 Come to Boise River Greenbelt. Pass through stile/cyclone fence. Turn right up short hill. Smooth asphalt now leads back to downtown.

23.3 Bear left at greenbelt fork to stay on main trail.

23.6 Go right off main greenbelt at Y.

23.7 Pass Natatorium pool and slide on right.

23.8 Turn left at Warm Springs Avenue. A generous bike lane is provided.

24.8 Turn right on Avenue C, just after cemetery on right.

25.0 Merge into Avenue D, and then bearing left, come to Reserve Street. Turn right onto Reserve Street and then make an immediate left on Scout. Follow Scout left around ball fields, where it meets Garrison and brings you back to completion of this almost Marathon ride at 25.3 miles.

Highland–8th Street–Camelback Loop

Location: Boise's north-end and foothills.

Distance: 4.9 miles.

Time: 30 to 60 minutes.

Tread: Pavement 2.3 miles; dirt/gravel road 0.9 mile; singletrack 1.7 miles.

Aerobic level: Intermediate.

Technical difficulty: 1 on pavement; 2 on road; 1 to 3+ on singletrack.

Hazards: Traffic on pavement and road; soft-sandy spots on road and singletrack; pedestrians in lower Hulls Gulch and at Camelback Park.

Highlights: You are at the center of Boise's north end at Camelback Park. To avoid crowds, go at off-peak hours and midweek.

Land status: Public.

Maps: Any Boise street map.

Access: From downtown Boise, take 13th Street north to Camelback Park. There is parking on 13th Street and at the park parking lot on Heron.

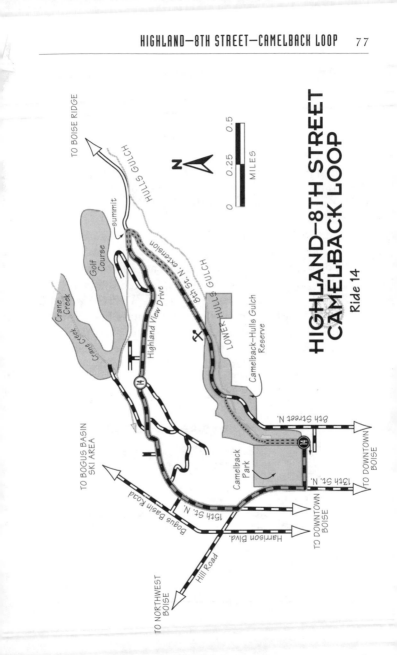

TO BOISE RIDGE

HULLS GULCH

N

0   0.25   0.5
MILES

HIGHLAND–8TH STREET CAMELBACK LOOP

Ride 14

Crane Creek

Golf Course

summit

Highland View Drive

8th St. N. extension

Crane Creek

LOWER HULLS GULCH

Camelback–Hulls Gulch Reserve

8th Street N.

TO DOWNTOWN BOISE

13th St. N.

TO DOWNTOWN BOISE

Camelback Park

TO BOGUS BASIN SKI AREA

Bogus Basin Road

15th St. N.

Harrison Blvd.

TO DOWNTOWN BOISE

Hill Road

TO NORTHWEST BOISE

The Ride:

0.0   From Camelback Park parking lot, go to 13th Street and follow it north (right) until it turns into Hill Road (at the northwest corner of Camelback Park).

0.2   Follow Hill Road northwest.

0.4   Turn right at 15th Street. Moderate grade.

0.8   15th Street turns into Highland View Drive. Grade steepens briefly.

1.3   Grade steepens again.

2.3   Come to end of Highland View Drive. Pavement ends; go to far-right end of cul-de-sac. Enter 8th Street through steel posts and turn right on 8th Street. Caution! This steep section of 8th Street is very soft and sandy, with occasional shutter bumps just to make things interesting. Motorheads, speed, and dust make this an extra special place!

2.6   Downhill grade flattens. Hulls Gulch (Trail 29) access is over bar gate to left. Stay right on 8th Street.

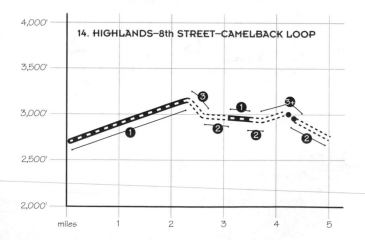

14. HIGHLANDS–8th STREET–CAMELBACK LOOP

2.9 On your right, a sandstone cliff and old quarry; on your left is the trail leading to Lower Hulls Grove Trail. (This trail will bring you to the junction, at 3.4 miles, and avoid traffic.)

3.2 Surface turns to pavement.

3.4 Turn right off 8th Street onto wide dirt trail that parallels 8th for a bit.

3.7 Bear right at 5-point junction. Cross creek just to right of pond. Bear right, going upstream a little, then climb a small hill that forks left, away from the creek bottom.

3.8 Bear right as trail flattens.

3.9 Bear left going up quick steep curve, a sustained short climb follows the side of the gully.

4.0 Saddle at trail tee. Turn left, gaining Camelback ridgetop. Views of downtown are unmatched from here.

4.1 Bear left at fork, keeping to ridge. Watch out for pedestrians, kids with boomerangs, and dogs pulling sweaty joggers. Ridge descends into saddle.

4.2 Just before saddle bottom (after steel post), hang a sharp left cutting back sidehill on the east side of the ridge. Caution! This is a narrow singletrack (4) with a sharp dip in it. Either go right and down (walking this section is advised due to the ruts) or follow the singletrack as it goes abruptly up and continues sidehill. Both options end up at the bottom, on the east side of the Camelback Ridge.

4.3 Turn right when you come to the east side main trail.

4.4 Pass through (around) a steel gate and bear right, keeping to the wide trail that hugs the south side of the Camelback.

4.7 Cross a descending trail hump and continue across the turf towards the tennis courts. Pass the courts and arrive at the completion of your loop in the parking lot.

NOTE: Lots of variations can be done within the park; once

you get to know your way around. Just remember—the downhill steeps should be done with care here; children are like ants and that picnic basket you're riding can be deadly.

Crestline—Mountain Cove Loop

Location: Lower foothills of the Boise Front, just north of downtown Boise.

Distance: 6.3 miles.

Time: 40 to 80 minutes.

Tread: Pavement 3.6 miles; gravel road 0.2 mile; doubletrack 1.6 miles; singletrack 0.9 mile.

Aerobic level: Moderate.

Technical difficulty: 1 to 3 on doubletrack; 2 to 3+ on singletrack.

Hazards: Traffic on Crestline Drive; some hoofbeaten doubletrack; and some quick-get-off-and-on-your-bike moves on a narrow, rocky singletrack.

Highlights: This is a wonderfully diverse ride that goes from wetlands to rugged ridges. It is also as close to downtown as you can get while still feeling like you are in the boonies. Most of it lies within the Old Fort Boise military reserve, where

CRESTLINE—MOUNTAIN COVE LOOP
Ride 15

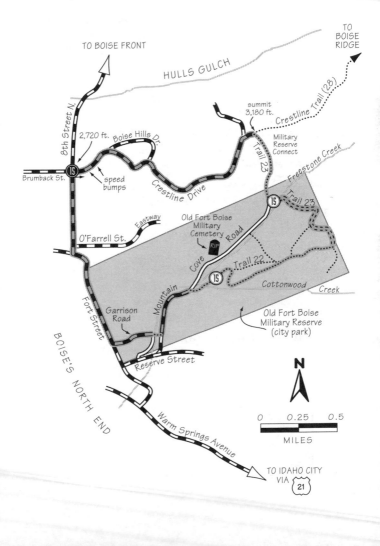

training and survival tactics have marked the land since Boise was first settled.

Land status: Public and some private.

Maps: USGS Boise North, Boise South, Ridge to Rivers.

Access: From Boise's North End, go to the intersection of 8th Street North and Brumback Street. The ride starts here.

The Ride:

0.0 From the corner of 8th Street and Brumback Street, head east on Brumback, which then merges into Boise Hills Drive. It is a gentle upward grade.

0.3 Turn right, up Crestline Drive.

0.4 Grade steepens, pavement narrows.

0.5 Hill crests; the road begins to wind.

0.9 Grade increases.

1.1 Grade increases.

1.3 View of Trail 23, down and to the right (your destination).

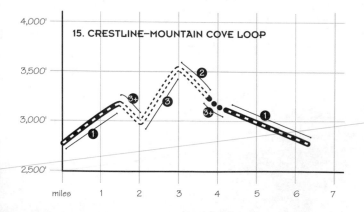

1.5 Turn right off Crestline. This is a wide, sandy access area.

1.6 Go right and down, around a metal gate on a doubletrack. This is the top end of Trail 23. Shift into your mid ring.

1.7 Bear left as the doubletrack hits fence line and turns to singletrack. This is a great section of trail—rolling, mostly smooth, and broken by rubber erosion skirts.

2.0 Hairpin turn; be wary.

2.2 Turn left and head up Mountain Cove Road (gravel).

2.4 The public part of Mountain Cove Road ends here (a private drive heads up to the left). Turn right at this point. Cross a stream (in spring, anyway), and before heading up the gravel road here, look to your immediate right. Trail marker 23 leads you off of the gravel and up a dirt doubletrack. Take a moment though, and check out the perfectly framed view of the Treasure Valley and the Owyhees in the distance. Then, with your eyes back to the trail at hand, note that the surface is quite hoofbeaten here, so pick your line and try not to think like a horse.

2.5 Shift to small ring; grade steepens.

2.6 Crest the hill. Bear right as the trail meets fenceline (The facilities you see ahead are the shooting range and clubhouse for the local "executive branch.") Trail winds up to the ridge on your right.

2.7 Gain ridge; grade eases.

2.9 Gain another higher ridge. Bear right on Trail 22, a well-defined doubletrack. A singletrack heads left and down toward the archery range. The vista here is 3/4 throttle; you can see about 270 degrees of the compass. Just below, you are looking into the Fort Boise Military Reserve, with Freestone Creek at its center. Trail drops quickly here. Watch out for ruts.

3.5 Keep left on doubletrack. A singletrack goes right here; this is Trail 22A, a short detour that comes back to the main trail.

3.7 Enjoy this section. It has great rollers and makes you feel like you could launch off this ridge and land on the U.S. Bank building (Idaho's tallest).

3.8 The trail leaves the ridge and switches back to the right, turning to singletrack and getting narrow. This is a bad erosion point where too many bikers have launched the ridge, leaving bad scars; please respect the closure. Sunflowers like this spot, signs of good things to come.

3.9 Switchback left; this is where 22A joins the main trail on the right. The trail gets narrow on the sidehill and has a quick, rocky section.

4.0 Turn right onto Cottonwood Creek Road at the bottom of Freestone Gulch. Cottonwoods and willows shelter this perennial oasis.

4.1 Take a left at Mountain Cove Road (the pavement resumes here) and either follow the road itself or, just ahead, break left to gain a levee road which parallels Mountain Cove Road on the left.

4.6 A BMX track is down and to your left: a fun little detour that will take you back to your 1-speed days. Turn right onto Reserve Street. Note: this BMX course may soon change to flood holding ponds, so look for signs.

4.7 Just after crossing the canal, take a dirt singletrack that leads to rough pavement and follows the north end of the Fort Boise ball fields.

4.8 Turn left at Garrison Road, which divides the ball fields from the tennis courts.

5.1 Turn right at Fort Street. This is the face of the Fort Boise complex.

5.6 Turn right at 8th Street North and ride back to its intersection with Brumback Street to complete this historic loop. And you didn't need a horse.

Eagle Ridge Loop

Location: Old Fort Boise Military Reserve, just north of downtown.

Distance: 5.1 miles.

Time: 30 to 50 minutes.

Tread: 2 miles on pavement; 1.3 miles on doubletrack; 1.8 miles on singletrack.

Aerobic level: Easy to moderate.

Technical difficulty: 2 on roads; 3 to 5 on singletrack.

Hazards: Other people, rocks, ruts, sand, and gravity.

Highlights: This is the closest singletrack to downtown. It covers some of the most varied terrain around.

Land status: Public

Maps: USGS Boise North, Boise South, Ridge to Rivers Trail System.

Access: From downtown Boise go north to the intersection of Fort Street and Garrison Road (the main entrance to Fort Boise Park). The ride starts from here.

The Ride:

0.0   From the intersection of Fort Street and Garrison Road pedal northeast (away from Fort Street) on Garrison,

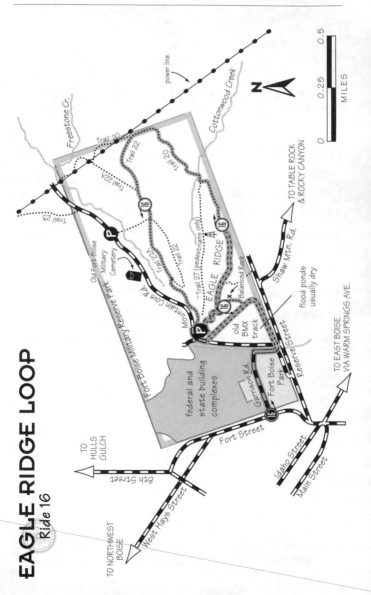

EAGLE RIDGE LOOP
Ride 16

passing the ball fields on the right. The pavement makes a right turn around the fields and deteriorates into gravel, this is Scout Lane.

0.4 Bear left on a singletrack through a stile, crossing a canal and Mountain Cove Road. Follow Reserve Street up a slight grade.

0.7 Go left at dirt road and through metal gate where Shaw Mountain Road veers off to the right from Reserve Street. Mostly flat and smooth now.

0.9 Go through metal gate, then immediately switchback up right through another metal gate, and head up moderate, winding hill. Surface is old pavement which is mostly good, but crumbling in spots. You are now on Eagle Ridge.

1.2 Grade levels and opens to views of downtown.

1.5 Pass radio facility on left. Come to end of pavement. Proceed on singletrack dirt where road leaves off.

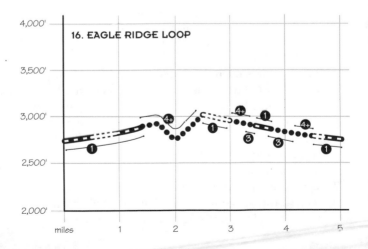

1.7 Grade drops; trail gets narrow.

1.9 Go right where singletrack splits, then right again on soft and narrow trail near the creek bottom. Trail to the left is pedestrian traffic only (Cottonwood Creek Trail 27).

2.0 Cross Cottonwood Creek and up to dirt cul-de-sac. To the left is the old archery range. Proceed across cul-de-sac to Trail 20 marker and up trail. This is a soft, sandy singletrack with some real steeps ahead! Begin climbing easily.

2.2 Soft and steep! Difficulty goes to 4+.

2.4 Once again, soft and even steeper. Difficulty 5.

2.5 Reach crest and summit of this ride. Take Trail 22 (middle fork), a doubletrack that heads level just west of downtown .

2.6 Grade down is moderately steep with soft spots and water bars.

2.9 Downhill eases.

3.0 Go right and down at singletrack fork . Then take left singletrack fork a few yards after. Trail goes sidehill in a fun, rolling line. This is Trail 22A.

3.2 Bear right and down at junction with Trail 22.

3.3 Go left at singletrack split. You're in the thick growth of Cottonwood Creek now. Soft pockets, tight turns, and blind corners push this section to a difficulty of 4+.

3.4 Come to dirt cul-de-sac. Go right on road and then, after 50 yards, left on Mountain Cove Road (pavement). The singletrack leading off to the left and across Cottonwood Creek here is pedestrian-only traffic. Swoop down Mountain Cove Road.

3.6 Cross Cottonwood Creek.

3.7 Go left at dirt/gravel road and up through gate that we went through before. Climb that paved hill again.

4.0 Go right at level dirt singletrack which heads east.

4.1 Take middle fork at split. Drop slightly to small saddle and up right to a rock prominence.

4.2 From this balanced rock (it is bigger on top than at its base) a choice of steep descents back to Fort Boise Park are visible. Many possibilities lie before you from this perch. Just be sure to be focused on the immediate descent from here; if you take the steeper route down the west side of this rock, you can have some extreme fun.

8th Street–Scott's Trail Loop

Location: Mid foothills of the Boise Front.

Distance: 6.4 miles.

Time: 60 to 90 minutes.

Tread: 2.8 miles county road (dirt/gravel); 0.4 mile doubletrack; 3.2 miles singletrack.

Aerobic level: Moderate.

Technical difficulty: 2 on road; 2-4 off road.

Hazards: All-terrain vehicles (ATVs); motorcycles on 8th Street; narrow singletrack in spots at upper end of trail; brush, rocky spots.

Highlights: This is a good example ride in the middle foothills (1,000–2,000 feet elevation above the valley floor below).

8th STREET–SCOTT'S TRAIL LOOP
Ride 17

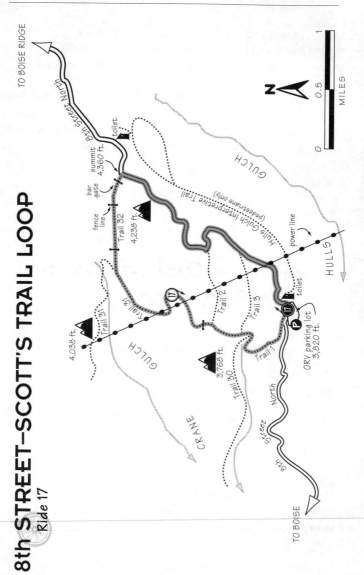

TO BOISE RIDGE

8th Street North

toilet

summit
4,360 ft.

bar
gate

fence
line

Trail 32
4,238 ft.

Hulls Gulch Interpretive Trail
(pedestrians only)

HULLS   GULCH

power line

Trail 31
4,038 ft.

Trail 1

Trail 2

Trail 3

toilet

CRANE   GULCH

3,768 ft.

Trail 30

Trail 1

ORV parking lot
3,820 ft.

P

8th Street North

4th Street North

TO BOISE

N

0   0.5   1
MILES

Although not particularly stunning in terms of scenic wonders, great views, good terrain variety, and an open airy feeling can be found here.

Land status: BLM and private land.

Maps: USGS Boise North and Robie Creek, Boise National Forest, Ridges to Rivers.

Access: From Boise's north end, drive north (up) 8th Street About 3 miles from the end of the pavement park at the ATV parking lot on right. The ride starts here.

The Ride:

0.0   Head northeast, up 8th Street, which is sand and rocks from here.

0.7   Pass under power lines.

0.8   Gain first crest. Grade dips, then eases.

1.0   Gain second crest. Dip and climb again.

1.1   Pass Trail 3 fork on left.

1.7   Pass Trail 2 fork on left. These two trails loop back to the lower part of this ride and may be closed in the future. Grade steepens at switchbacks.

2.1   Gain third crest. Grade eases.

2.8   Turn left onto Trail 32. Descend short, steep singletrack through low bar gate. Grade eases.

3.4   Trail leaves ridge and follows narrow sidehill. Watch out for rocky-rollies in trail rut and ankle-biting sage.

3.6   Pass through remnants of a barbed wire gate and fence. A sign will inform you that you are entering private land.

3.7   Regain ridge as the slope eases.

3.8   Pass switchback that cuts down to the right; this is the way to the Corrals and Bogus Basin Road. You are now on Trail 31.

3.9   Climb knob. Track widens.

4.1   Descend ridge. Trail turns to doubletrack with rocky sections.

4.5   Trail narrows to singletrack with water bars.

4.8   Climb over ridge and down.

5.2   Go through BLM gate; you're back in the public domain. Doubletrack resumes.

5.3   Descend to open draw: Trail 2 forks left up steep hill. Trail 1 picks up here.

5.6   Arrive at Crane Creek saddle. Trail 30 forks right (Bob's Trail follows Crane Creek down); go right on Trail 1 as it winds across the hill and climbs. It is a wide singletrack leading around a final knob, back to the start of this ride.

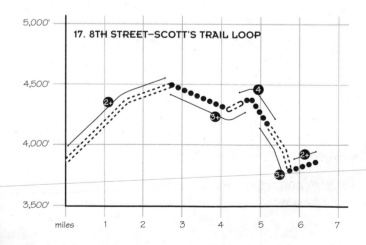

Hulls Gulch–Crestline Trail

Location: Lower Boise foothills.

Distance: 7.7 miles.

Time: 60-90 minutes.

Tread: 2.4 miles pavement; 2.2 miles dirt road/doubletrack; 3.1 miles singletrack.

Aerobic level: Moderate.

Technical difficulty: Pavement 1; doubletrack 2+; singletrack 2-4+.

Hazards: Traffic on Crestline Drive; pedestrians; zooming bikers on singletrack (especially in the gulch on some tight, blind turns); rocks, boulders, stream crossings and occasional narrow sidehill trail in the upper end of the gulch. Probably the most heavily used trails in the foothills (Trail 28 is Crestline; Trail 29 is Lower Hulls Gulch), you're more likely to run into (literally) other trail users on this loop than anywhere else in the area. For this reason alone, it's a good idea to stay away during peak hours, weekends, and holidays.

Highlights: This is one of the central trails in the lower foothills; it branches off to at least 3 other Ridges to Rivers trails. Although the upper gulch is a bit of a pump and relatively technical, there are no killer hills. The descent down Crestine Trail is loads of fun, pretty smooth, and provides chances for BMX-style moves.

HULLS GULCH–CRESTLINE TRAIL
Ride 18

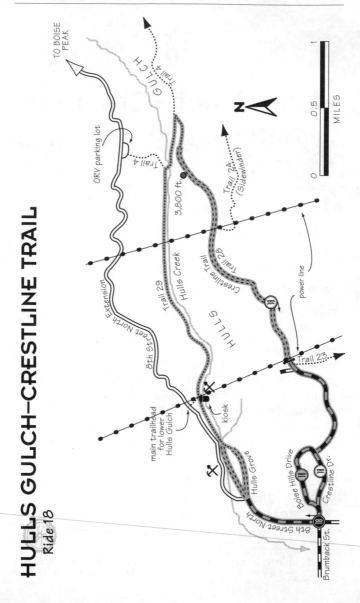

Land status: Public and private.

Maps: USGS Boise North, Boise National Forest, Ridge to Rivers Trail System.

Access: In Boise's north end, drive to the intersection of Brumback Street (Brumbaugh) and 8th Street North. The ride starts here. There is parking 3 blocks away at Camelback Park.

The Ride:

0.0 From the corner of Brumback Street and 8th Street North, ride north up 8th Street.

0.7 Turn right at dirt pullout. Pass through a metal post (open) gate and continue up smooth, wide paths leading under locust and other shade trees. The paths diverge not too far after the gate; take either one because they converge shortly. This is Hull's Grove, the lower, treed part of Hulls Gulch.

1.0- **Option:** For a shorter loop, take this new singletrack right as it climbs gently.
     1.2 Wind through a dip then go right as singletrack splits; climb moderately with a few short steeps. Left here will lead to new parking area on 8th Street.
     2.0- Go right on Cresline, Trail 28. Descend wide singletrack. In 0.1 mile, come to mile 5.9 on the original ride. Left at Trail 23 will take you into the Military Reserve.

1.0 Bear left and cross Hulls Creek.

1.1 Come to 8th Street (sandy, gravel). Follow it briefly. Go past private road on right and end of barbed wire fence.

1.3 Take first singletrack trail right; leave 8th Street.

1.4 Cross creek, left. Smooth, sandy surface with occasional rocks.

1.5 Take fork right or left. Left will bring you back closer to

8th Street; both will converge again shortly.

1.6   This is the main Hulls Gulch trailhead for people going into the higher reaches. Trail kiosk is close to the road. Continue up singletrack that follows creek bottom.

1.7   Sand pocket.

1.8   Rollers (round rock). Grade increases slightly.

2.0   Prepare to cross creek after a sharp, banked splash.

2.1   Cross creek again.

2.3   Grade steepens.

2.4   Short, steep section, then a dip. Downshift to get boost for narrow tricks and rollers.

2.5   Burst up another short steep grade.

2.8   Thin sidehill trail; get off balance in the wrong spot and you are in the creek.

3.1   Pass sign; enter BLM land. Look up left to see some craggy formations.

3.2   Carry around rock outcropping; creek makes a sharp bend here. Blind curves just beyond; beware the DOS (descending outlaw speedster).

3.6   Trail junction. Trail 4 heads up and to the left (it joins

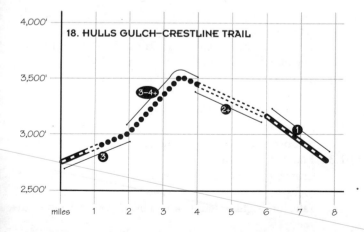

18. HULLS GULCH–CRESTLINE TRAIL

8th Street at the ORV parking lot after a 0.5 mile climb). Bear right and cross creek; you've now left Trail 29 and joined Trail 28. This is also the summit of this ride; shift into your middle ring.

3.7 Trail smooths out and widens; first vista of Boise and the Owyhees to the south.

3.9 What was just sidehill of the ridge you have been following now opens up. Pass Trail 4 on left. Keep to main doubletrack that descends easily through a sandy base. Lots of fun to be had on this section where banked turns, jumps, and fun thin lines abound.

4.7 Pass Trail 24 on left; gain ridgetop.

4.8 Ridge widens and drops into a saddle. Doubletrack veers off right (and hugs ridge around knob). For a great vista though, bear left up singletrack (the upper trail) to knob top. Regain main trail by zooming around the knob south to the obvious doubletrack.

5.9 Go through metal gate. Trail 23 is just past here on the left. Proceed on level through sandy parking/trail access area.

6.0 Turn left at pavement (Crestline Drive), a 25 mph, rough-surface, winding asphalt road. (There's an option here to go right at pavement. This takes you to the end of a cul-de-sac where a sandy trail veers off to the right. This then leads to a singletrack which descends left from a small saddle. Referred to by locals as the "Back Door," this dirt trail leads to Boise Hills Drive. Note: The Back Door may become Phase II of Somerset Ridge, so watch for closures.)

7.0 Either stay on Crestline Drive or turn right here on Boise Hills Drive. They converge in 0.5 mile.

7.5 Follow Boise Hills Drive right, down and out; it turns into Brumback Street, which takes you back to 8th Street and our starting point.

Crestline–Curlew Ridge Loop

Location: Boise Front foothills, northeast of downtown Boise.

Distance: 15.7 miles.

Time: 2 to 3.5 hours.

Tread: Paved 5.4 miles; Gravel/dirt road 0.5 miles; doubletrack 7.9 miles; singletrack 1.9 miles.

Aerobic level: Strenuous.

Technical difficulty: 2 to 4+ on doubletrack and singletrack.

Hazards: Steep, rocky, and soft sections. Steep ascents require pushing your bike in places; ruts, rocks, and soft spots (sometimes all coinciding) may require walking the steep downhill. Four-wheel drives have pushed this route beyond what is civilized. Watch for seasonal or changing closures.

Highlights: An excellent view of Rocky Canyon, some exposure. If you like big hills, this is a ride for you. A great mixture of rolling over smooth ground, rocky grunts, and urbane pavement.

Land status: Public and private.

Maps: USGS Boise North, Boise South, Robie Creek; BLM Boise Front, Ridge to Rivers.

Access: Go to the intersection of Fort Street and Garrison Road, just north of St. Luke's Medical Center on the eastern edge of

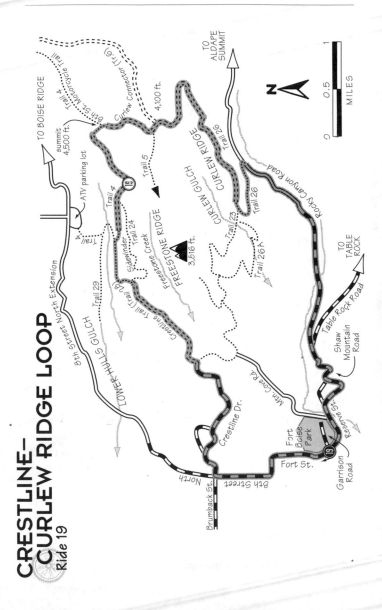

CRESTLINE—
CURLEW RIDGE LOOP
Ride 19

downtown. This is the main entrance to Fort Boise Park and Recreation Center. Parking is available along the ball fields and around the tennis courts.

The Ride:

0.0 From the intersection of Fort Street and Garrison Road go northwest on Fort Street, minding the traffic.

0.5 Turn right on 8th Street, heading north. Do not miss the cultural center of the north end—the Boise Co-op—on your left, just after you turn onto 8th Street. 8th Street rises gently; two sets of speed bumps.

1.1 At Brumback Street turn right.

1.2 Brumback Street turns into Boise Hills Drive; follow up moderate rise.

1.4 Bear right up Crestline Drive. Hill becomes steep quickly.

1.6 Grade crests momentarily, road narrows. If you like *Sunset* magazine covers, you will love this neighborhood, but don't let the landscaping delude you—watch out for 40 mph Cabriolets and Acuras.

2.6 Turn right off Crestline Drive into a wide, sandy access area.

2.7 From the turnout at the top of Crestline Drive, go through a metal cable/gate and follow the doubletrack. This is Trail 28 (Crestline Trail, or as some locals call it, The Freeway). Gentle to moderate climb and a mostly smooth surface lie ahead.

3.1 Hit soft pocket, then short steep hill; grade then mellows.

4.0 Pass Trail 24 (Sidewinder Trail) junction on right. Trail turns to singletrack.

4.8 At trail junction (marked by wooden rails) turn right and go up. This is Trail 4, which initially climbs steeply. It is narrow with some blind curves.

5.4 Reach saddle and trail junction. Take middle track, which is a singletrack that heads down and straight towards Table Rock in the distance (south). The upper end of Trail 24 is on your right. A steep, rocky doubletrack heads up to the left; it is usually closed. Watch out for sheep grazing in this area.

5.6 Ascend steep, doubletrack ridge.

5.9 Another steep and brief crest.

6.1 Cross under power lines.

6.3 Trail crests again.

6.7 Turn right at junction. Follow Trail 6. From ridgetop, the summit of the ride at 4500 feet, descend.

7.3 Cross under power lines.

7.4 Bear left at junction. Trail 6 marker may or may not be there.

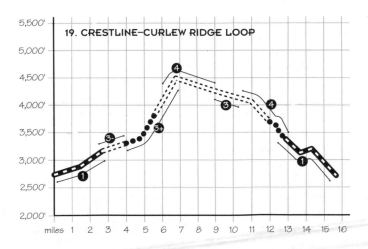

7.8 Cross creek and climb. There are small granite buttresses here and switchbacks.

8.2 Trail crests, shift into mid ring. Boogie to get up short steep section.

8.3 Caution! This section is a series of 2 short, steep knobs with equally steep backsides. When you come off the tops, be ready for ruts, rocks, and your opposite karmic personality coming the other way.

8.4 Bear right at closed trail junction on left. Trail and grade mellow briefly here.

8.9 Another steep climb.

9.1 Hit ridgetop saddle; go right at junction. This is a steep and rocky section.

9.4 Go up steep, short knob and down a steep, rocky track.

9.7 Come to fenceline and bear right at doubletrack, keeping to ridge; this is now Trail 26. (A wide grassy trail leads off to the left towards Rocky Canyon, now visible to the left.)

10.2 On Curlew Ridge, cross under power lines and large, colored Bamba Balls!

10.9 Great views of Rocky Canyon and Curlew Ridge spires.

11.0 Go down dip and bear right around ridge. Descent quickens.

11.6 Gain open, grassy ridge and view of Table Rock to south and Boise Valley to the southwest. Go left and down Trail 26, a doubletrack heading toward Rocky Canyon and east. (Upper end of Trail 26A, Shane's Trail, goes to the right here.)

11.7 Trail switchbacks left, follow.

11.9 Short, steep downhill.

12.0 Lower leg of Trail 26A heads right (south). Stay to main doubletrack as you bottom out in small gully and start to rise. Climb two small rises.

12.1 Gain a small saddle and bear left onto a new

singletrack, keeping to Trail 26, which goes steep and narrow for the next 0.4 mile.

12.3 Tricky, tight curves, dips, and rocks in narrow sidehill section puts this at 3+ for technical difficulty.

12.4 Trail goes steeply down as you approach Rocky Canyon Road and the end of Trail 26. It is not a bad idea to walk here if things are the least bit soggy. At Rocky Canyon Road go right (southwest) and down a gentle gravel surface. Watch out for traffic (all kinds). Also, be sure not to miss the basalt spires and crags in the mouth of Rocky Canyon.

12.9 Come onto pavement. Nice cruising ahead.

13.7 Cross Cottonwood Creek, then cattleguard, and begin climbing moderate hill.

14.2 Rocky Canyon Road turns to Shaw Mountain Road as you gain crest. Bearing right, follow Shaw Mountain Road as it winds its way down and back to Boise proper. (Table Rock Road cuts off to the left and east here.) Watch out for some narrow and tight curves ahead; this is not a good place to test the compatibility of residential traffic and downhill speed.

15.2 Shaw Mountain Road turns into Reserve Street. Downhill grade diminishes at curve.

15.4 Just after passing Mountain Cove Road to the right, turn right off Reserve Street onto a dirt singletrack. Bearing right, this short trail leads to the east side of the Fort Boise Park ball fields.

15.5 Following this deteriorating surface (Scout Lane) around a corner to the left and better pavement, you're now on Garrison Road. Follow Garrison back to its intersection with Fort Street to complete this 15.7-mile loop.

Rocky Canyon Road

Location: Boise Front, east of downtown Boise.

Distance: 13 miles.

Time: 2 to 3 hours.

Tread: 2.6 miles paved road; 10.4 miles dirt/gravel road.

Aerobic level: Moderate to strenuous.

Technical difficulty: 1 on pavement; 1 to 2+ on gravel.

Hazards: Traffic, shutter bumps, and sandy spots.

Highlights: This is some of the prettiest terrain in the Boise Front. For most of the way, the road is followed by Cottonwood Creek; you're seldom more than a stone's throw from the water. Climbing-quality crags (up to about 100 vertical feet) seem to jump out at you. At Aldape Summit, you are at the treeline (where the conifers start, not stop). You might even nurture the fantasy (as you smell the firs) that you are in the Pacific Northwest.

Land status: Public access road. Access off of the main road is restricted to specific uses in most places.

Maps: USGS Robie Creek; BLM Boise Front, Boise National Forest; Ridge to Rivers.

Access: From downtown Boise at the northeast end, follow Reserve Street north to Shaw Mountain Road. Follow Shaw Mountain to where it splits into Table Rock Road. At this juncture (to your left), Shaw Mountain Road becomes Rocky

ROCKY CANYON ROAD
Ride 20

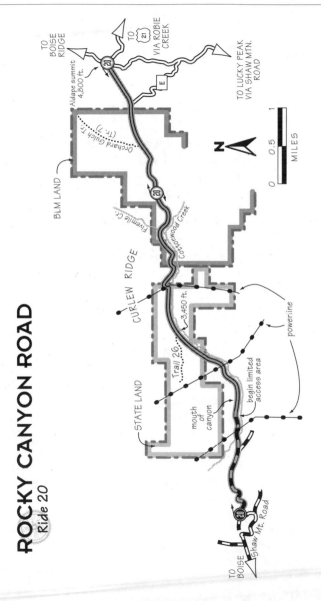

Canyon Road. The ride starts here. There is limited parking available, but please be careful where and how you park; this is a residential area.

The Ride:

0.0 Start from the bottom of Rocky Canyon Road (it starts where Table Rock Road splits from Shaw Mountain Road). This is a small crest, so the pavement here gets you off to a nice, easy-gliding cruise.

0.4 Exercise caution as you go over cattle guards and dip down to cross Cottonwood Creek.

0.5 Begin a winding and rolling climb.

1.3 Pavement ends. Road bears left up steeper grade.

1.6 This is the mouth of the canyon. Large rock crags tower over the road. Some of the rocks are climbing-quality, with the most striking formations jutting directly over Cottonwood Creek

1.8 Pass (on left) an old ORV trail that is now closed. The severe rutting is a testimonial to the power of the motorhead. A steel barricade discourages present use.

1.9 Pedal past a new Ridge to Rivers singletrack trail on the left: Curlew Ridge/Gulch 26

2.5 Pass through a creek-bottom grove of cottonwood, willow, and locust. The shade is welcome, even in the spring.

2.9 Pass under the big, colored Bamba Balls (one-meter, aerial spheres on high spans of transmission wires) that span the canyon. Take a left at the pullout here to view an interesting rock totem.

3.1 At the Public Lands (BLM) marker, the grade steepens.

3.85 Pass steel gate and cable on left. Fivemile Creek enters the canyon here.

4.7 Pass a gated, private road on the right. You are now in a burn area, which continues for almost a mile.

4.8 Just before a 20-foot-high granite hoodoo, a doubletrack heads off to the left; pass on by.

5.2 Doubletrack goes left with gate and marker. This is Orchard Gulch.

5.7 Doubletrack veers off to left, to follow creek; this is another entrance to Orchard Gulch.

5.8 Doubletrack goes right, crosses Cottonwood Creek and leads into fir trees. This road connects with the Shaw Mountain Road and leads over into the Deer Creek drainage above Lucky Peak Reservoir. Keep to the main road.

6.3 Junction of Rocky Canyon and Shaw Mountain roads. Bear left on Rocky Canyon Road and start climb to Aldape Summit. The grade steepens.

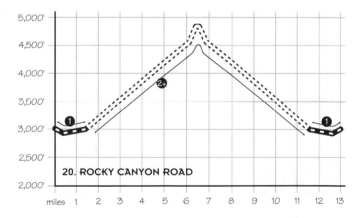

20. ROCKY CANYON ROAD

6.5 Aldape Summit; hike up the little knob on your right to gain a full vantage. The Sawtooths are visible to the east-northeast; the Trinitys are just visible to the east. Boise Ridge to the north even offers a granite face. Catch your breath and return the way you came to complete this tour of one of the Boise Front's little gems.

Crestline-Sidewinder Loop

Location: Boise Front lower foothills, just north of downtown.

Distance: 8.6 miles.

Time: 60-75 minutes.

Tread: Pavement 3 miles; dirt doubletrack 1.8 miles; singletrack 3.8 miles.

Aerobic level: Moderate.

Technical difficulty: 1 on pavement; 1 to 2+ on doubletrack; 2 to 4+ on singletrack.

Hazards: Traffic, driveways, and downhill speed on Crestline Drive; soft spots, rocks, ruts, and dagger-like sagebrush in places off road. This is a well-traveled trail; watch out for hikers, other bikers, and horses, too!

Highlights: The Sidewinder Trail section of this loop (Trail 24)

CRESTLINE-SIDEWINDER LOOP
Ride 21

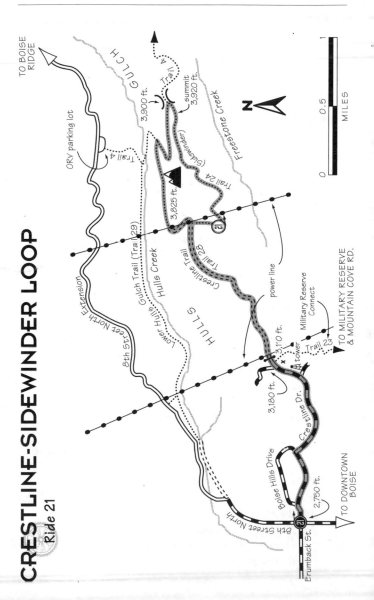

is the most technical part; there is exposure and quick, steep climbs with equally quick descents. Steering a fine line can make all the difference on this trail. The Crestline Trail (Trail 28) is a popular route; a good place to check out the latest fashions/equipment in the mountain biking milieu.

Land status: Public and private.

Maps: USGS Boise North, Boise National Forest, BLM Off-Road Vehicles on the Boise Front, Ridge to Rivers.

Access: In Boise's north end, go to the intersection of 8th Street North and Brumback Street. The ride starts from here.

The Ride:

0.0   From the corner of 8th Street North and Brumback Street head east up Brumback. It turns into Boise Hills.

0.1   Brumback turns into Boise Hills Drive.

0.3   Pavement forks; take right up Crestline Drive. Boise Hills Drive continues left.

0.4   Gentle rise gets serious; shift into low ring.

0.5   Grade crests and levels, road narrows. This neighborhood is one continual *Sunset* magazine cover.

1.1   Vista to lower left of Hulls Gulch Trail.

1.4   Vista to upper right is Shaw Mountain (terraced); to lower right is Trail 23.

1.5   Turn right off Crestline Drive into a wide access area (an unofficial parking lot).

1.6   Trail 23 is to the right and down. Stay left and go through or under metal gate-cable. You are now on Trail 28, the Crestline Trail (also known as The Freeway). Soft, rutted doubletrack ascends ridge gently.

1.9   Get some momentum; this is a short, steep hill. May be deeply rutted.

2.1 Gain ridgetop; grade levels. Fun rollers follow.

2.3 Trail forks; stay right (more traveled doubletrack).

2.4 Trail becomes singletrack. Take Trail 24 (Sidewinder) right. Pass under power line.

2.5 Sidehill trail can be deeply pocked with hoofprints. Winding, rolling, and narrow, and closely surrounded by brush, in the spring, this section seems like a sea of sage.

3.1 Climb gently through a switchback, under a powerline, and gain ridgetop. East Boise opens up below.

3.3 Bear right; grade steepens.

3.6 Slope levels, trail widens.

3.8 Pass through remnants of a BLM gate. Vista to lower left of Hulls Gulch/Trail 4 junction. Climb short, steep nob, then quick dip and crank in your granny gear to gain another.

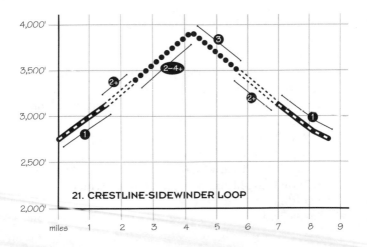

21. CRESTLINE-SIDEWINDER LOOP

4.0 Trail splits, bear right.

4.1 Bear right again; this next nob is hauntingly similar to the last two, but, due to the exfoliated granite, it is both rocky and sandy at once. Enjoy it while you exercise butterfly-like balance.

4.2 This small rise is this loop's summit (elevation 3,920 feet). Go down a slight dip.

4.3 Reach a saddle and junction with Trail 4, which runs both left and right. Descend fork left, but stay in a low gear; you'll need it for some quick rises. Caution: The next quarter mile drops relatively quickly; it's narrow, bumpy, and exposed in places. Tire-biting ruts add to the adventure.

4.9 Come to junction with Trail 28 (no trail marker/sign at this date, but you'll know it by the wooden rails on the upper side of the junction). Bear left; you're now on Crestline Trail again. Trail smooths and eases. Fun rollers, bankers, and football-sized nuggets call for total immersion.

5.7 Widens to doubletrack; pass Trail 24 turnoff on left. Track turns soft and sandy.

6.5 Slow! Brake for a short, steep, and deeply rutted section. Stay right.

6.9 Cross back under the metal gate/cable.

7.0 Join Crestline Drive and turn left at pavement. Shift into your big ring. Caution! Limited visibility around curves and blind driveways make for a dangerous combination with this beckoning grade.

7.3 If your eyes aren't too bleary, check out the vista south of west Boise and the Owyhees.

7.9 Boise Hills Drive dives off to the right here. If you take it, you'll avoid a stop sign where it merges with Crestline Drive.

8.3 Merge with Brumback Street. Follow to 8th Street and comlpete loop. Come back to Earth through Boise's bohemian north end, which is not quite all the way back, thankfully.

Barber–Warm Springs Loop

Location: Barber Flats, a few miles east of Boise.

Distance: 7.6 miles.

Time: 35 to 65 minutes.

Tread: Paved greenbelt (bicycle and pedestrian pathway) and paved road.

Aerobic level: Easy.

Technical difficulty: 1.

Hazards: Traffic on greenbelt; crossing Warm Springs Avenue.

Highlights: This easy loop, just east of Boise, hugs the rimrock leading to the Boise River Canyon. Just south of the route is the Boise River–Barber Flats Wildlife Management Area. Views of the river on one side and the buttes on the other provide great bird watching and geology viewing. This section of the greenbelt is also heavily traveled, so it's a great social loop. Families with bike trailers will find this route safe and enjoyable, year-round.

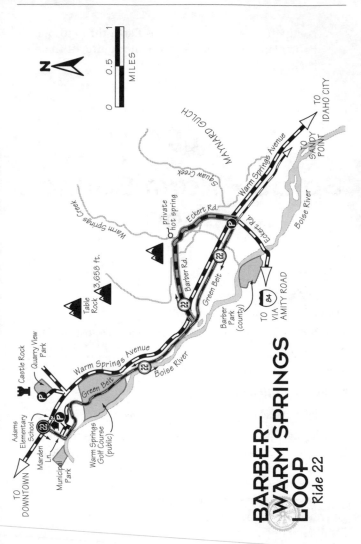

BARBER–
WARM SPRINGS
LOOP
Ride 22

Land status: Public pathway and county roads.

Maps: USGS Boise South, Lucky Peak; Ridge to Rivers Trail System; any good Boise city map.

Access: From the intersection of Broadway and Warm Springs Avenue, go east onWarm Springs about one mile. On the right (south) will be Adams Elementary School flanked by The Natatorium (just east and behind) and Marden Lane (just west of Adams). There is parking at the "Nat" parking lot and, to a limited degree, on Marden Lane. The ride starts on the corner of Warm Springs Avenue and Marden Lane.

The Ride:

0.0   Go south, down Marden Lane on a paved pathway. The Natatorium Complex is to the left (east).

0.1   Go left at the junction with the main Boise River greenbelt. Head through poplars and into the golf course district. Be aware that this section of the greenbelt (for this entire ride) gets lots of use; you will meet 'bladers, bikers, runners, and strollers, so keep your head up!

0.3   Bear left at the greenbelt junction; this is where a new section of pathway will connect with the Park Center district of town, just south and across the river. Warm Springs Public Golf Course begins straight ahead.

0.4   Ignore a couple of paved lefts that lead off into neighborhoods. Stay to main path.

1.0   Stiles and pathway stop sign warn of main golf course crossing. Golfers have the right-of-way. Begin a gradual rise.

1.6   A rock wall to the left defines the grade difference as Warm Springs Avenue rises away from the greenbelt.

The riparian zone is now squeezed up against you as you hug the river.

1.8 Private drive crossing. Caution!

2.3 Turn left, off of the greenbelt, where Warm Springs Avenue rejoins the pathway. Cross the highway and head up East Barber Drive (also known as Barber Road), rising slightly.

2.7 Crest a small hill and pass Showa Koi Fish Farm on your left. You are now in the middle of the Warm Springs thermal aquifer

2.9 Dip, before climbing a small hill (the biggest of this ride).

3.1 Crest the hill (the highpoint of this ride).

3.2 Enter Warm Springs Gulch. If you look up the gulch a hundred yards or so, you may see a steam plume rising from (guess what?) Warm Springs Creek. All around is the Harris Ranch, surrounded by white rail fences (a huge development is planned for this site, some time in the near future).

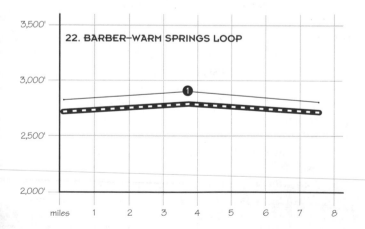

3.3 Cross Warm Springs Creek and descend a gentle, rolling grade.

3.6 At this right-angle curve, Barber turns into Eckert Road. Follow the main road.

4.0 Cross Warm Springs Avenue—Caution! This is a congested area and motorists may be cranking. After crossing, go right (west) onto the greenbelt. You are now heading back toward Boise. Although this is a flat section, there is a prevailing headwind here.

4.8 Private crossing.

4.9 Private crossing, again.

5.2 Pass Barber Road–greenbelt exit-point on right. Stay on main pathway.

5.7 Private crossing.

6.5 Golf crossing.

7.2 Go straight through 4-way junction. Stay on the main pathway.

7.4 Go right onto a paved path and up Marden Lane. Climb a small rise to starting point at Warm Springs Avenue.

Castle Rock Loop

Location: East Boise foothills.

Distance: 2.7 miles.

Time: 20 to 30 minutes.

Tread: Pavement 0.3 mile; doubletrack 0.7 mile; singletrack 1.7 miles.

CASTLE ROCK LOOP
Ride 23

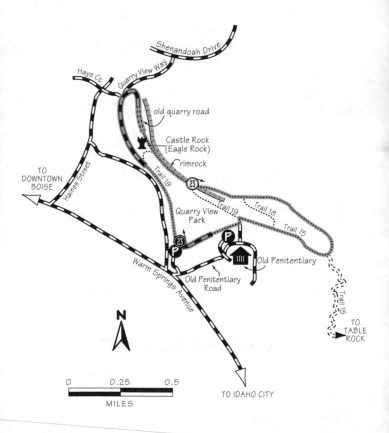

Shenandoah Drive

Hays Ct.

Quarry View Way

old quarry road

Castle Rock
(Eagle Rock)

rimrock

TO
DOWNTOWN
BOISE

Haines Street

Trail 19

23

Trail 19

Trail 18

Trail 15

Quarry View
Park

23

P

P

Old Penitentiary

Warm Springs Avenue

Old Penitentiary
Road

Trail 15

TO
TABLE
ROCK

N

0   0.25   0.5

MILES

TO IDAHO CITY

Aerobic level: Beginner/intermediate.

Technical difficulty: 1 to 2 on doubletrack; 2 to 3 on singletrack.

Hazards: Rocky, narrow singletrack in spots.

Highlights: Affording great views of east Boise and the Front Range, this short loop around Castle Rock offers a range of rocky trails and ridge riding.

Land status: Public and private.

Maps: USGS Boise South, Boise city street map.

Access: From downtown Boise, go east on Warm Springs Avenue, 1.4 miles. Turn left on North Penitentiary Road, then take an immediate left again, which will take you to Quarry View Park. The ride starts in the parking lot.

The Ride:

0.0 From the Quarry View parking lot, pedal north on sidewalks through the park.

0.1 Just past the jungle gym and a line of Russian olive trees at the park boundary, get onto one of two singletrack trails that lead toward Castle Rock (obvious rock crag just north).

0.2 Bear left (west) along an ill-defined, grassy singletrack that hugs the hillside beneath Castle Rock.

0.3 Steepening hillside merges with new fill road. Push up onto road and follow sidehill to left.

0.6 Intersection of East Hays Court and Quarry View Way. Follow Quarry View uphill on smooth pavement.

0.7 Turn right on Castle Rock Court and follow to end.

0.8 Look for trail leading off to the right; take it. You are now on an old quarry road (doubletrack). Grade is moderate as road leads to Castle Rock, just under rock rim.

1.1 Doubletrack ends, turns to narrow and rocky singletrack.

1.2 Saddle above Castle Rock. Go left, uphill, to reach a trail that switches back to the right, continuing gently up towards Table Rock.

1.4 Gain ridgetop. Bear right on sandy trail that heads east towards Table Rock.

1.5 Bear left and down on doubletrack that leaves ridgetop.

1.7 Cross private road and continue on ill-defined doubletrack that leads through grassy meadow.

1.9 Go through opening in barbed wire fence. Signs indicate no motor vehicles. Turn right just beyond fenceline. At this point, you are on Trail 15 heading west toward the old penitentiary.

2.0 Bear left at first split in trail. Then, perhaps 40 yards beyond, bear right at trail fork where sign indicates bikes to right, pedestrians to left.

2.2 At Trail 15 marker, go left, then immediately right, down a short, steep fork to singletrack leading west above Warm Springs pumphouse.

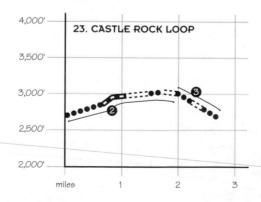

2.3 Bear right on doubletrack leading uphill. Follow old road along bench.

2.4 Pass old reservoir on right. At end of old reservoir shoot down short steep grade to enter meadow and return to Quarry View Park.

Table Rock Lower Loop

Location: Northeast Boise foothills.

Distance: 4.9 miles.

Time: 40 to 80 minutes.

Tread: Doubletrack 2.4 miles, singletrack 2.5 miles.

Aerobic level: Moderate.

Technical difficulty: 1 to 2 on doubletrack, 1 to 5 on singletrack.

Hazards: Pedestrians, other bikers on trails. Some very rocky and narrow trail sections; a couple of spots where the trail width narrows to a rocky notch that must be pushed or carried over. Also some bad ruts in places. Beware of the active quarry.

Highlights: Despite its proximity to downtown and its popularity with locals and tourists, this is one of the premier rides in the Boise Front. The rocky ruggedness of the terrain combines with crows nest views of the Boise Valley and the city

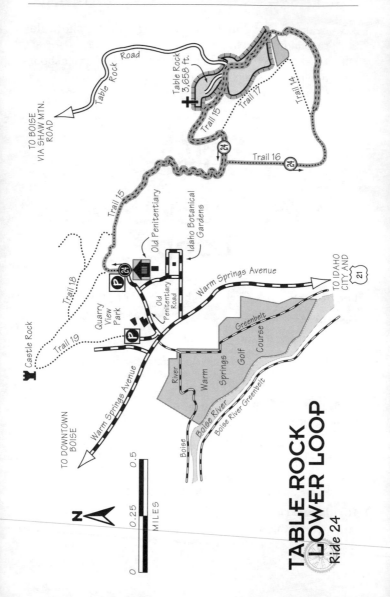

TO BOISE VIA SHAW MTN. ROAD

Table Rock Road

Table Rock 3,658 ft.

Trail 15

Trail 17

Trail 14

24

Trail 16

24

Trail 15

Old Penitentiary

Idaho Botanical Gardens

TO IDAHO CITY AND

21

Trail 18

24

Warm Springs Avenue

P

Quarry View Park

Old Penitentiary Road

Castle Rock

Trail 19

P

Warm Springs Avenue

Greenbelt

Warm Springs Golf Course

TO DOWNTOWN BOISE

River

Boise River

Boise River Greenbelt

Boise

N

0   0.25   0.5

MILES

TABLE ROCK LOWER LOOP

Ride 24

itself to make this little ride seem big in some ways. Great picnic and rock climbing potential along the way. The Old Penitentiary, administered by the Idaho State Historical Society, is a wonderful place to investigate. Tours and info available year-round, across the street from the guard house.

Land status: Mostly public and some private.

Maps: USGS Boise South, BLM Boise Front, Boise National Forest, Ridge to Rivers Trail System.

Access: From downtown Boise, go east on Warm Springs Avenue. Turn left on North Penitentiary Road and left again when you see the sign for the Idaho Botanical Gardens (there will be a small sign in the middle of Penitentiary Road pointing left for Group, RV, and Bus parking). This will lead around behind the Bishop's House to a gravel parking lot. The Bishop's House is the more ornate of only two Victorian homes on the Old Pen grounds. It was home to the prison's bishop and was located in town when the bishop lived there. The house may be rented for weddings, parties, etc. The ride starts from here.

The Ride:

0.0   From the northeast corner of the parking lot behind the Bishop's House (near the Guard House) head uphill to the Trail 15 (Table Rock) trailhead. A singletrack leads up left (a sign indicates pedestrians only to the right).

0.1   Trail climbs and switchbacks to east; there are some tricky rocks to negotiate.

0.3   Pass Trail 18 junction on left. Stay to right on Trail 15. Surface and grade eases.

0.5   Keep to right as trail comes in from left. The doubletrack leads from draw up a winding sidehill ascent.

0.8 Pump this steep and rutted section!

1.1 Take singletrack Trail 16 (Table Rock Loop) to the right. You are on a rise now, and the trail heads off and down gently under power lines.

1.2 Singletrack meets doubletrack as you bear right.

1.4 Trail turns to singletrack again. Go through a narrow, rocky section that descends into a draw. Don't be too proud to walk this unless you're made of neoprene.

1.5 Hit doubletrack, bearing left and down. It becomes a singletrack that is steep and rocky briefly.

1.7 Just after a sharp dip, go left at doubletrack. This is the old quarry road used to haul the stone down to the penitentiary. Climb this moderate but increasing grade.

1.9 Trail forks, go right, which heads up a sidehill.

2.0 Get speed up for dip and quick left up a short, steep hill.

2.2 Bear right where two trails divide in a Y.

2.3 Follow doubletrack up and right around interesting flatiron-like boulders.

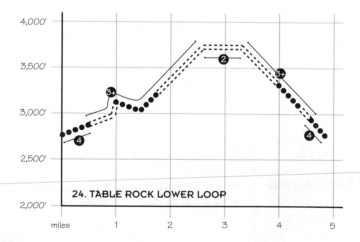

24. TABLE ROCK LOWER LOOP

2.4 Pump this short dip and then up a steep section.

2.5 Pass through double metal gate and continue up sustained doubletrack hill. There's a sign here indicating no motor vehicles beyond this point. Local sponsors of this access are listed, so when you get a chance, please show your support.

2.6 Gain ridge; bear left up steep doubletrack to the eastern prow of Table Rock rim. Just a bit further and you are at the quarry itself. Please stay out of the quarry as it can be active. (Things like explosives and heavy machinery may be hazardous to your health.)

2.7 Follow switchback to right, which leads up around the back (north) side of Table Rock rim. Trail narrows as you get near the top. The rocks converge into a narrow notch, and unless you have leaping bike, this is a carryover. On top, bear right on dirt roads towards communications towers.

3.0 At the junction with Table Rock Road (you'll go through a boulder barricade), go left.

3.1 Just behind microwave towers and fenced facility, take the dirt road right toward downtown Boise.

3.2 At rim, bear right on doubletrack, toward cross.

3.3 Come to draw with Trail 15 marker. Take this rocky and steepening singletrack down, which leads off under the cross.

3.6 Switchback cuts left. This is an interesting grassy spot with a natural rock wall.

3.7 Trail 17 leads off as a singletrack to the left here. Continue down on Trail 15, bearing right. Watch out for bad ruts and steep section ahead.

4.6 Keep to the left on Trail 15 at junction with Trail 18. The trail then splits, directing pedestrians to the left and bikers to the right; stay to the right. Follow singletrack down narrow and rocky slope back to the parking lot and completion of loop. The most stylish way to finish is to pick the sage from your teeth, the cheatgrass from your socks, and, if you're timing is right, wander through one of the many receptions at the Bishop's house, spilling champagne, and mingling with the tiger shrimp.

Table Rock Loop

Location: Boise Front foothills, just east of Boise.

Distance: 5.3 miles.

Time: 40 to 80 minutes.

Tread: 2 miles on pavement; 0.7 miles on singletrack; 2.6 miles on doubletrack.

Aerobic level: Easy.

Technical difficulty: 2 to 4 on singletrack; 1 to 2 on doubletrack.

Hazards: Runaway joggers (with dogs) on pavement, children on battery-driven vehicles, rocks, ruts, washboard roads, and carousers in pickups.

Highlights: A great view of Table Rock's prow, including the cross and the communications towers; a social smorgasbord of the upper east end.

Land status: State land, public and private roads. Please be aware when crossing the private land here; keep to the main

TABLE ROCK LOOP
Ride 25

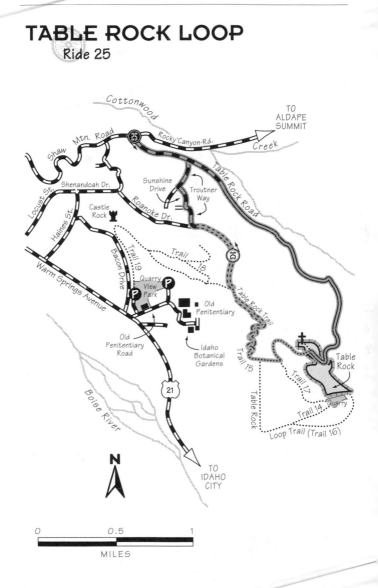

Cottonwood

Creek

TO
ALDAPE
SUMMIT

Shaw Mtn. Road

Rocky Canyon Rd.

25

Table Rock Road

Locust St.

Shenandoah Dr.

Sunshine
Drive

Troutner
Way

Castle
Rock

Haines St.

Roanoke Dr.

Trail 19

Trail
18

25

Bacon Drive

Quarry
View
Park

P

P

Old
Penitentiary

Table Rock Trail

Warm Springs Avenue

Old
Penitentiary
Road

Idaho
Botanical
Gardens

Trail 15

Table Rock

Trail 17

Table Rock

Quarry

21

Trail 14

Loop Trail (Trail 16)

Boise River

N

TO
IDAHO
CITY

0   0.5   1

MILES

trail and ride courteously. Permission to pass here may be re-voked.

Maps: USGS Boise South; BLM Boise Front; Ridge to Rivers Trail System; any good street map of Boise.

Access: From downtown Boise go east on Reserve Street until it turns to Shaw Mountain Road. Follow Shaw Mountain up a little more than a mile to its intersection with Table Rock Road on the right. The ride starts from here.

The Ride:

0.0 From the junction of Table Rock and Shaw Mountain roads head up (east) Table Rock Road. It is an easy to moderate climb up smooth pavement.

1.1 Surface turns to gravel, grade steepens. Suburban arrival gives way to natural semi-arid terrain. Soft pockets and washboard call for skill in picking a line. Also remember, this is a party road; do not let it spoil yours.

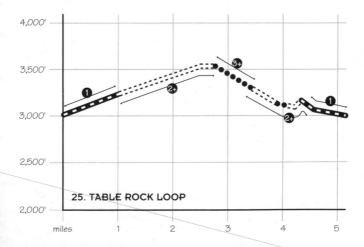

25. TABLE ROCK LOOP

1.5 Grade eases.

1.9 Crest and glide.

2.1 From dip pump up steep section again.

2.5 Bear right at Table Rock plateau. Head for the cross; a dead-end dirt road heads just left of it.

2.6 At rim follow singletrack left and slightly down.

2.7 Go right and down doubletrack, then make a quick, sharp right again a singletrack that drops quickly and roughly. This is Trail 15 (Table Rock Trail).

3.0 Switchback left at twin rock walls. Grade eases.

3.2 Trail 16 is marked to left. Stay right on Trail 15 and watch for center rut.

3.3 Suface mellows. Trail goes doubletrack.

3.9 Bear right and up slightly on singletrack as you reach a grassy draw. This takes you away from Trail 15, through a fence line, and onto private land. Bear right again when you reach a doubletrack split.

4.0 Follow doubletrack to a small rise.

4.1 Bear right on gravel road, descending slightly.

4.4 Come to pavement. This is the junction of Troutner Way and Roanoke Drive. Go right (up) Troutner on smooth pavement.

4.7 Go right again where Troutner meets Sunshine.

4.9 Turn left at Table Rock Road, a smooth glide.

5.3 Complete loop at Shaw Mountain Road junction.

Castle Rock–Table Rock Loop

Location: Northeast Boise foothills

Distance: 6.2 miles

Time: 50 to 70 minutes.

Tread: Doubletrack 1.6 miles; singletrack 4.6 miles.

Aerobic level: Moderate.

Technical difficulty: 2 to 3 on doubletrack; 2 to 5 on singletrack.

Hazards: Take the usual hazards that tourists, bikers, pedestrians, and errant youth offer, compound them with steep and exposed trails and rocky surfaces (both loose and bedrock; sometimes combined), and you have a great place to injure yourself. If you want to go fast here, let the reminder of the old state pen slap you out of your urge for anarchy. Please note that although some of the old Table Rock Quarry may be now open, a part of the quarry is active (you know, heavy machinery, blasting). There are ample signs to warn you away, but when in this area, be especially aware and alert.

Highlights: The flip side of the coin is that all of the liabilities suggested also make this a great place to bike. Sandstone steps (from 3-foot-high to your Japanese garden variety), bedrock with marbles and sand lightly sprinkled throughout, and knife-edge pathways that narrow to ankle-crushing dimensions all

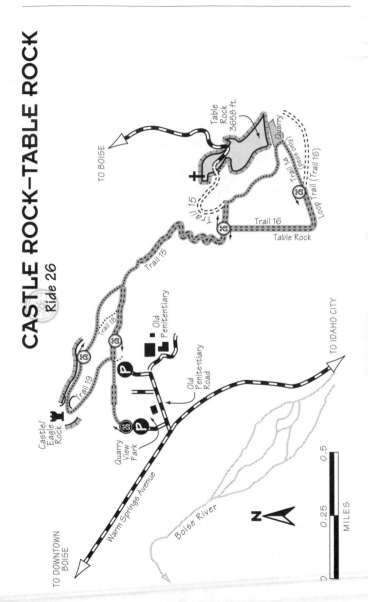

CASTLE ROCK–TABLE ROCK
Ride 26

TO BOISE

Table Rock 3658 ft.

Quarry

Trail 14 (pass only)

26

Loop Trail (Trail 16)

Trail 15

26 Trail 16

Table Rock

Trail 15

Trail 18

Trail 19

26

26

Castle/ Eagle Rock

Old Penitentiary

Old Penitentiary Road

P

26 P

Quarry View Park

Warm Springs Avenue

TO DOWNTOWN BOISE

TO IDAHO CITY

Boise River

N

0   0.25   0.5
MILES

can be encountered here. Yes, they can be safely negotiated. There are also ideal opportunities for picnicing and rock climbing in many spots.

Land status: Mostly public, some private.

Maps: USGS Boise South, BLM Boise Front, Boise National Forest, Boise city street map, Ridge to Rivers.

Access: From downtown Boise, go east on Warm Springs Avenue. Turn left onto North Penitentiary Road, then take another immediate left (paved) which leads to Quarry View Park. The ride starts from the parking lot.

The Ride:

0.0 From the Quarry View Park parking lot pedal north (toward Castle Rock, which rises abruptly behind the park) through the park and past the jungle gym, through a line of shade trees (Russian Olives) and onto one of two singletrack trails that lead through a wild grassy meadow.

0.1 Turn right at a more defined singletrack that rises slightly to the east.

0.2 Climb a bump and you are on a doubletrack.

0.3 Stay left; follow the singletrack uphill and above the Warm Springs Pumphouse.

0.4 Take singletrack left uphill. After you gain a main trail heading to the left sidehill, stay left and climb quickly. You are on Trail 19 now. To the right is Trail 15, leading off to Table Rock. This narrow, quickly rising section has some fixed rock obstacles (3).

0.8 Gain shoulder just above Castle Rock. Check out the view from the rock prominence for an eagle's perspective (it's also known as Eagle Rock). Then bear right up a singletrack that cuts sidehill back to the right and under the rim rocks. Exposure on right.

1.1   On top of the ridge now are rock rooms, walls, and holes to drop into; here, the trail splits. Keep generally to the right, following main ridge trail; there are occasional, small signs to assist you. Big steps and drops in places!

1.3   Go left past the Trail 18 junction marker, which points right. Descend bedrock strewn with marble-sized gravel.

1.4   Merge with Trail 15; go left, climbing through a grassy draw.

1.6   Climb a doubletrack winding uphill.

1.9   Steep grade and ruts make this a tricky pump.

2.1   Stay left and bypass the Trail 16 marker on your right. Rutted doubletrack steepens again.

2.3   Bear right (up) at singletrack leading off sidehill. This is Trail 17 (not marked this time) and it is very

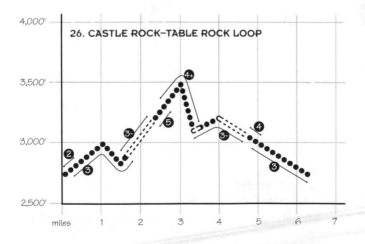

technical (technical difficulty 5); loose rocks, fixed rocks, steeps, and narrow passages through brush all contribute to the thrill (pain) of it.

2.5 Trail opens up and eases. Sandstone boulders give way to bigger rocks on left.

2.7 Go through an old fence line and around a rock corner, and the scene changes: this is part of the old quarry. A true rock garden, 40-foot dihedrals of granite-quality sandstone rise up; a broken table, 15 feet thick, creates a cave. This is a magical spot, whether you climb or not.

2.9 Trail fractures as it hits the rubble boundary nearing the active quarry. This is the summit of the ride. Stay to the right of, and just below the quarry road that comes down from the top of Table Rock. Danger and Keep Out signs define the restricted area. Exit the rubble via a sharp switchback to the right, heading downhill. This is an old quarry road that drops steeply (Trail 14—not marked at this time). This trail is closed to bikes, so walking your bike is not only prudent but required.

3.0 Exposed on left, with big rocks and steep grade.

3.3 Meet Trail 16; stay right on Trail 16 doubletrack. Grade eases considerably.

3.4 Go right up a steep singletrack sidehill and under power lines.

3.6 Ascend a rocky draw and up a steep, rocky singletrack on the right. A jeep road splits off to the left here.

3.7 Sage and sandstone give way to a cruising dip down and up.

3.8 Follow to the right of a fence line.

3.9 Bear left on singletrack where it splits from a road going right.

4.0 Turn left on Trail 15 at the marker and junction. Descend rutted and winding doubletrack.

4.6 Bear left in draw where another trail splits off to the right.

4.7   Bypass the rocky trail heading uphill to the right (with Spanish-style house above) and continue down Trail 15 briefly to next trail branching right. This is Trail 18; the first section is steep bedrock with sandstone steps cut for pedestrians.

4.8   Go left where the Trail 18 marker indicates right; this is a trickier, more aesthetic line which hugs the rim.

5.0   Veer right to gain main trail on top of ridge, heading west.

5.2   Trail splits; bear left on bedrock towards downtown. Leave ridgetop on sidehill trail.

5.5   Bear left on Castle Rock shoulder to gain Trail 19 down, your way up.

5.8   Stay right, going downhill as you pass the Trail 15 junction on your left. Follow trail back west to return to Quarry View Park and the completion of the loop.

West Highland Valley—Cobb Trail Loop

Location: East Boise foothills.

Distance: 6.7 miles.

Time: 90 to 120 minutes.

Tread: 0.8 miles on pavement; 0.7 miles singletrack; 5.2 miles doubletrack.

WEST HIGHLAND VALLEY–COBB TRAIL LOOP
Ride 27

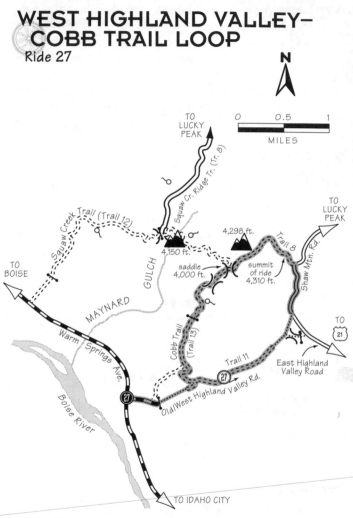

N

0   0.5   1

MILES

TO LUCKY PEAK

Squaw Cr. Ridge Tr. (Tr. 8)

Squaw Creek Trail (Trail 12)

TO BOISE

MAYNARD GULCH

4,150 ft.

4,298 ft.

Trail 8

TO LUCKY PEAK

Shaw Mtn. Rd.

saddle 4,000 ft.

summit of ride 4,310 ft.

Warm Springs Ave.

Cobb Trail (Trail 13)

Trail 11

TO 21

East Highland Valley Road

Boise River

27

27

Old/West Highland Valley Rd.

TO IDAHO CITY

Aerobic level: Moderate to strenuous.

Technical difficulty: 1 to 4 off pavement.

Hazards: Crossing Warm Springs Avenue (from parking area); sustained steep sections with a variety of surface surprises including marble- to cantaloupe-sized loose rocks, hoof-beaten clay (the hardness of concrete), and soft pockets hidden beneath the weeds. Closed January 1 through April 1 for wintering deer and elk.

Highlights: This ride is a vertical sprint; there is very little cruising or easy trail. Even the descent is tricky. You may like this kind of character-building diversity. Views of the East Boise Valley, a shady spring, and solitude are less spartan benefits.

Land status: State and private.

Maps: USGS Lucky Peak, BLM Boise Front, Boise National Forest, Ridge to Rivers Trail System.

Access: From downtown Boise head east on Warm Springs Avenue. Just past the Crow Inn (on the right) West Highland Valley Road (paved) branches left; continue on Warm Springs Avenue past the turn, then pull off the road and park on south side. There are a couple of dirt roads that converge here, and the greenbelt is accessible from here, too. Cross Warm Springs Avenue to go north on West Highland Valley Road; the ride starts from here.

The Ride:

0.0   From the intersection of Warm Springs Avenue and West Highland Valley Road, pedal north up a gentle slope, passing houses in a subdivision on the right.

0.4   Pavement turns to gravel.

0.6   Come to an ill-defined cul de sac. Scattered outbuildings and no trespassing signs give this place a private and confused look. Go past the large steel gate. Trail 11 (West Highland Valley) is marked here. Doubletrack is rough and bumpy, and climbs at a moderate pace.

0.9   Bear right where Trail 13 forks left; this keeps you on Trail 11, climbing, climbing.

1.0   Go through rocky slide section. This section (difficulty 5) is a walk for most.

1.1   Golfball- to softball-sized rocks; continue climbing.

1.5   Hill gets real steep now. Ruts and smoother surface now; steering a fine line becomes an art form on this stretch with a difficulty of 3 (and keeps you on your bike).

1.8   Go around old cattleguard.

2.0   Bear left (north) on singletrack (difficulty 3+) that climbs up away from main doubletrack. This shortcut is a quicker, more interesting way to gain the ridge. There is a tricky center rut and some hard surface.

2.3   Reach saddle, dip, and then bear left on Shaw Mountain Road (E Trail). Climb smooth but occasionally steep sections.

3.0   Go left on Squaw Creek Loop Road (Trail 8). Road is smooth, except for a cattleguard, as it dips, then switchbacks west and up to summit of ride. This is summer cattle range. Caution! You don't want to buy more steak than you can eat by middle age. Shift to your middle ring. This is the best cruise of this ride.

3.9   View of eastern Boise Valley. Caution! Steep, rocky slopes coming up. How about a steep climb over sand and rock?

4.2   Go left at Trail 13 (Cobb Trail) marker down moderate doubletrack ridge that turns rocky.

4.3   Grade becomes severe (some exposure in places). Difficulty exceeds 3 and pushes 4.

4.6   Bear left and down main trail, into small saddle.

Difficulty mellows to -2 .

4.8 Bear right at spring, following draw. This small grove of locust, ash, and willow is a nice shady rest spot. Whether a camp or a dwelling, this was somebody's home at one time. The trail here is an easy glide.

5.4 Go left at Trail 13 marker. (Main trail looks like it goes right here, but that route, although simpler, crosses private land.)

5.7 Descent becomes rocky and steep. Drop into gully.

5.8 Cross creek/gully bottom and climb up the other side. This is a loose and tricky section.

5.9 Go through barbed wire gate (two hands to close) and then go right and down Trail 11. Left is up and the way we ascended. Shift to your middle ring.

6.2 Come to Trail 11 head (steel gate), pass private home.

6.4 Reach pavement and zoomer zone.

6.7 Complete loop at Warm Springs Avenue.

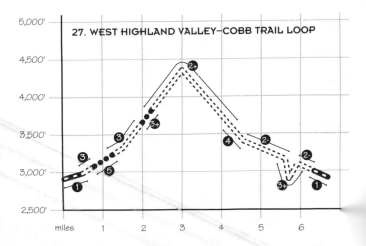

Squaw Creek–Cobb Trail Loop

Location: Boise foothills, east of downtown.

Distance: 8.6 miles.

Time: 90 to 120 minutes.

Tread: 5.6 miles doubletrack; 0.5 miles singletrack; 2.5 miles pavement.

Aerobic level: Strenuous to moderate.

Technical difficulty: 1 on pavement; 2 to 4 on doubletrack; 3 on singletrack.

Hazards: Traffic crossing Warm Springs Avenue; cattleguards; soft and rocky steep sections. Some sections of the ride can be badly hoof-printed (cows, this time). This area is closed from January 1 through April 1 for wintering deer and elk.

Highlights: Good training for the bigger rides, views

Land status: Idaho Fish and Game, BLM

Maps: BLM Boise Front, USGS Lucky Peak, Ridge to Rivers Trail System.

Access: From the intersection of Idaho and Warm Springs Avenue (at the east entrance of St. Luke's Regional Medical Center), go east on Warm Springs Avenue 5.2 miles. Turn left into Squaw Creek Road and drive to the end of the pavement. The ride starts from here.

SQUAW CREEK—COBB TRAIL LOOP

Ride 28

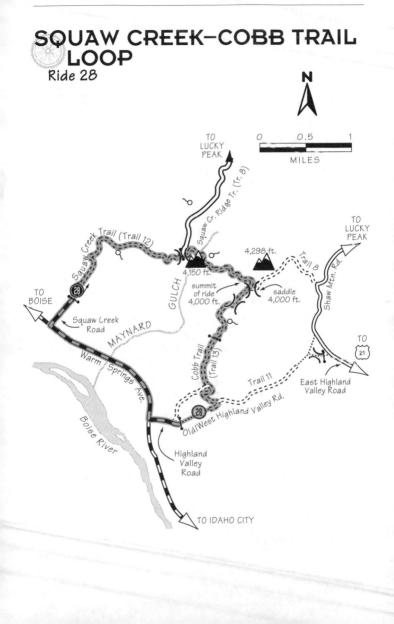

The Ride:

0.0 Head north from the end of Squaw Creek Road on doubletrack. Go through metal gate. Trail 12 (Squaw Creek) is marked. Grade is gentle to begin with.

0.4 Trail steepens quickly, levels at creek bottom, then steep climb continues. This section is rutted, and good balance in granny gear helps.

0.9 Pass old locust grove and spring on left .

1.1 Climb a series of 3 short steep sections accompanied by dips (no, not your friends).

1.5 Gain ridge and vista south to Owyhees. Grade eases.

1.6 Steep sections and dips continue. Switchbacks lend to the fun.

2.1 Steep climb continues, and surface also turns to sand.

2.2 Come to metal gate. Turn right on Trail 8 (marked) and drop down over a cattleguard. Shift into your middle ring; this is one of the few cruising parts of this ride as the trail descends moderately.

2.7 The honeymoon is over; another series of quick, steep climbs with dips for relief.

3.5 Steep climbs continue; it gets sandy, too.

3.7 Gain ridge, then saddle. At Trail 13 (Cobb Trail) turn right and go down. This is the summit of this ride. This trail hugs the ridge, but also goes just sidehill. Grade drops quickly here with some very soft and rocky sections combined.

4.1 Reach saddle; bear left and down. Old gatepost and 8-foot bitterbrush here suggest the spirit of Clint Eastwood in an old spaghetti western. Trail mellows in grade and surface.

4.4 Trail narrows to singletrack. Go by old spring, trough, and locust grove. This spot looks like it might have been a homestead once. It is an oasis if you are riding in the summer heat.

5.0   Go left at Trail 13 marker. Descend.

5.4   Cross gully bottom and climb out rugged 2-track.

5.5   Go through wire gate and right, down Trail 11.

5.8   Pass through steel gate. Follow Highland Valley Road.

6.5   Come to and cross Warm Springs Avenue. Jog left about 10 yards and follow dirt road down to Boise River Greenbelt.

6.6   Turn right as you enter the greenbelt; follow the rolling, smooth ribbon west.

7.5   Greenbelt meets Warm Springs Avenue. Stay on Greenbelt.

8.0   Pass Boise Parks and Recreation Department.

8.1   Pass Boise Front National Forest Office.

8.3   Turn right off greenbelt and cross Warm Springs Avenue. Head north up Squaw Creek Road, climbing gentle grade to the end of the road, the ride, and the completion of the loop.

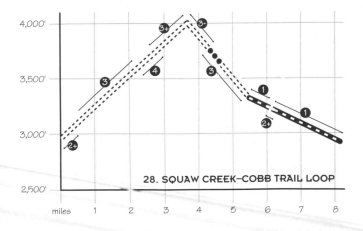

28. SQUAW CREEK–COBB TRAIL LOOP

Highland Valley–
Squaw Creek Loop

Location: East Boise Front.

Distance: 9.9 miles.

Time: 90 to 120 minutes.

Tread: 2.3 miles on pavement; 6.1 miles doubletrack/dirt road; 1.5 miles singletrack.

Aerobic level: Moderately strenuous.

Technical difficulty: 1 to 4+ off pavement.

Hazards: Crossing Warm Springs Avenue (Old Highway 21); rocky sections (loose and fixed), soft, sandy pockets. Trail 8 (Squaw Creek Ridge), Trail 11 (West Higland Valley), and Trail 12 (Squaw Creek) are closed January 1 through April 1 for wintering deer and elk.

Highlights: The steep uphill sections of this ride are concentrated in the second quarter. The descent is steep and bumpy, but totally rideable. If you are in shape, this loop is a skilled sprint.

Land status: State, BLM, public, and a small section of private from 9.1 to 9.6 miles.

Maps: USGS Lucky Peak, BLM Boise Front, Boise National Forest, Ridge to Rivers.

HIGHLAND VALLEY— SQUAW CREEK LOOP
Ride 29

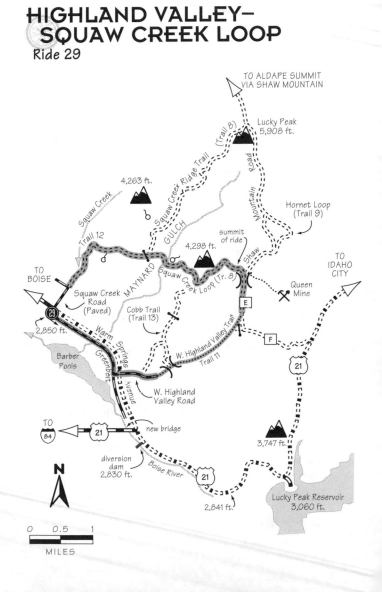

TO ALDAPE SUMMIT
VIA SHAW MOUNTAIN

Lucky Peak
5,908 ft.

Squaw Creek Ridge Trail (Trail 8)

Hornet Loop
(Trail 9)

4,263 ft.

Squaw Creek

Trail 12

GULCH

summit
of ride

4,298 ft.

Mountain Road

Shaw

TO
BOISE

MAYNARD

Squaw Creek Loop (Tr. 8)

TO
IDAHO
CITY

Queen
Mine

29

Squaw Creek
Road (Paved)

Cobb Trail
(Trail 13)

E

2,850 ft.

Warm Springs

Greenbelt

W. Highland Valley Trail
Trail 11

F

21

W. Highland Valley Road

Barber
Pools

Avenue

TO
84

21

new bridge

3,747 ft.

diversion
dam
2,830 ft.

Boise River

21

Lucky Peak Reservoir
3,060 ft.

2,841 ft.

N

0   0.5   1
MILES

Access: From downtown Boise go east on Warm Springs Avenue 5.3 miles from its start at Broadway. Turn left onto Squaw Creek Road and park. Some limited shady spots are available just up Squaw Creek Road. The ride starts from the intersection of Warm Springs Avenue and Squaw Creek Road.

The Ride:

0.0 From the intersection of Warm Springs Avenue and Squaw Creek Road, pedal southeast on greenbelt (south of Warm Springs Avenue).

1.7 Turn left off greenbelt. Go through cyclone fence/stile. Head up short, steep doubletrack that leads to Warm Springs Avenue.

1.8 Cross Warm Springs Avenue and head north up Highland Valley Road (paved).

2.0 Grade increases.

2.1 Pavement turns to gravel.

2.3 Come to an ill-defined cul-de-sac. Scattered outbuildings and no trespassing signs give this place a private and confused look. Go through boom gate. Trail 11 head is marked. Doubletrack is rough and bumpy, and climbs briskly.

2.6 Trail 13 is on left. Stay right and uphill; this keeps you on Trail 11, Highland Valley Road, which degrades into singletrack for the next mile. Get ready to climb!

2.7 Go through rocky slide section. Difficulty goes to 4+.

2.9 Rocky section and some exposure as track hugs right edge. Continue climbing.

3.3 Hill goes steep now. Ruts and smoother surface makes balancing a line tricky.

3.6 Go around old cattleguard.

3.7 One more steep!

3.8 Go left up singletrack that climbs sidehill. This section is hummocky and rutted with hoofprints to rattle your brain. Difficulty pushes 3+.

3.9 Grade eases.

4.0 Reach saddle.

4.1 Drop onto Shaw Mountain Road (dirt) and bear left, uphill.

4.2 Big granite eggs on right. Climb a series of steeps with intermittent respites.

4.8 Turn left off Shaw Mountain Road (Trail E) and onto Squaw Creek Loop (Trail 8). Just past this small crest go over cattleguard and down slight grade. Climb a series of switchbacks with soft, sandy pockets.

5.2 Reach crest and summit of this ride. Follow smooth and winding dirt road through a summer range area. Use caution and try not to spook the "slow elk."

5.7 Caution! Nose down steep ridge; it's rock covered with sand in spots. Views into Maynard Gulch deserve a look.

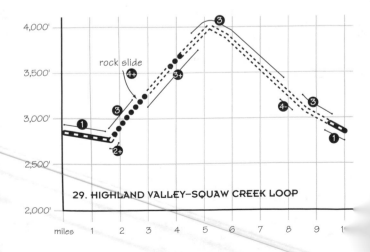

29. HIGHLAND VALLEY—SQUAW CREEK LOOP

6.0   Trail 13 is to left. Stay right on doubletrack (Trail 8) and down.

6.5   Cross small gully, then climb out.

6.7   Round ridge and swoop down again.

7.1   Pass spring at gully bottom, then climb up steep and out.

7.4   Go through fenceline, cattleguard, then left at marked gate. This is Trail 12, a doubletrack which drops quickly. To the right ,Trail 8 continues up to Lucky Peak. View of East Boise Valley is free.

7.6   Caution! Steep downhill with sharp, rocky curves. But then get going for small uphill.

8.0   Pass spring on left: locust trees, vines and trough.

8.2   Steep, rocky, and rutted downhill section as you enter gully.

8.4   Shade is available here: locust and willow, but watch out for poison ivy.

8.6   Pass old homestead remains on right: locust trees and shade.

9.1   Go through metal gate; stile is on left.

9.2   Bear left where gravel road splits; right goes to private mobile home.

9.4   Go through fenceline, cattleguard and past Fish and Game signboard on right.

9.6   Go through metal gate/fenceline and onto pavement of Squaw Creek Road. Glide down to Warm Springs Avenue to complete loop.

Highland Valley– Lucky Peak Dam Loop

Location: East Boise Front.

Distance: 10.2 miles.

Time: 90 to 120 minutes.

Tread: 6.9 miles on pavement; 1 mile singletrack; 2.3 miles doubletrack/dirt road.

Aerobic level: Moderately strenuous.

Technical difficulty: 2 to 4+ off pavement.

Hazards: Crossing and cruising Highway 21; high weeds; rocky sections (loose and fixed); soft, sandy pockets on the initial descent. Trail 11, West Highland Valley Trail, is closed January 1 through April 1 for wintering deer and elk.

Highlights: Virtually all the uphill vertical is in the first 2.5 miles; the remainder of the trail is a cruise. The ascent is isolated (your sweat is private); the descent is social (gliding and cruising are public).

Land status: State, BLM, public.

Maps: USGS Lucky Peak, BLM Boise Front, Boise National Forest, Ridge to Rivers.

HIGHLAND VALLEY– LUCKY PEAK DAM LOOP
Ride 30

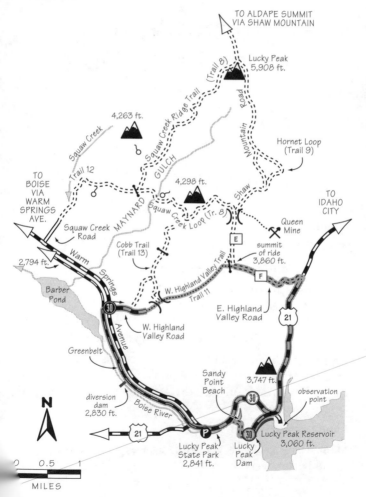

TO ALDAPE SUMMIT
VIA SHAW MOUNTAIN

Lucky Peak
5,908 ft.

(Trail 8)

Squaw Creek Ridge Trail

Mountain Road

4,263 ft.

Squaw Creek

Trail 12

MAYNARD GULCH

Hornet Loop
(Trail 9)

4,298 ft.

TO BOISE VIA WARM SPRINGS AVE.

Squaw Creek Loop (Tr. 8)

Shaw

Queen Mine

Squaw Creek Road

Cobb Trail
(Trail 13)

E

summit of ride
3,860 ft.

TO IDAHO CITY

2,794 ft.

Warm Springs

W. Highland Valley Trail
Trail 11

F

21

Barber Pond

30

W. Highland Valley Road

E. Highland Valley Road

Greenbelt

Avenue

3,747 ft.

30

observation point

diversion dam
2,830 ft.

Boise River

Sandy Point Beach

21

P

30

Lucky Peak Reservoir
3,060 ft.

N

Lucky Peak State Park
2,841 ft.

Lucky Peak Dam

0   0.5   1

MILES

Access: From downtown Boise head east 6.8 miles on Warm Springs Avenue. Just past the Crow Inn (on the right) Highland Valley Road (paved) branches left; stay right. Immediately past the turnoff, park on the south side of the highway. A couple of dirt roads converge here, and the greenbelt is accessible from here, too. Cross Warm Springs Avenue to go north on West Highland Valley Road; the ride starts from this intersection.

The Ride:

0.0 From the intersection of Warm Springs Avenue and Highland Valley Road, pedal north up a gentle slope, passing houses in a subdivision on the right.

0.4 Pavement turns to gravel.

0.6 Come to an ill-defined cul-de-sac. Scattered outbuildings and no trespassing signs give this place a private and confused look. Go through boom gate. Trail 11 head is marked. Doubletrack is rough and bumpy, and climbs briskly.

0.9 Bear right where Trail 13 forks left; this keeps you on Trail 11, Highland Valley Road, which degrades into singletrack for the next mile. Get ready to climb!

1.0 Go through rocky slide section. Difficulty goes to 4+.

1.1 Golfball- to softball-sized rocks, some exposure on right. Continue climbing.

1.5 Hill gets real steep now. Ruts and smoother surface prevail; steering a fine line becomes an art form (and keeps you on your bike).

1.7 Steep again.

1.8 Go around old cattleguard.

1.9 Last severe hill!

2.0 Bear right (east) on doubletrack that climbs and winds up rocky draw.

2.2 Gain saddle and summit of this ride. Go through boom gate, and bear left (downhill). Trail turns to doubletrack/dirt road.

2.3 Come to junction with Shaw Mountain Road (designated Trail E) and bear right, downhill. You are now on the eastern part of Highland Valley Road.

2.8 Downhill grade increases, with soft pockets to make it interesting. As you approach gully bottom, gain speed for uphill cruising ramp.

3.1 Repeat scene similar to 2.8: steep descent, speed through bottom, and up smooth.

3.4 Come to small crest and Idaho Fish and Game sign and kiosk. Lucky Peak Reservoir and Idaho Highway 21 are visible down to the southeast. Cross cattleguard and continue east on Highland Valley Road.

3.7 Turn right at Highway 21 and head down long, smooth grade. Caution! Cars and trucks come whipping down this grade and there is not a lot of shoulder.

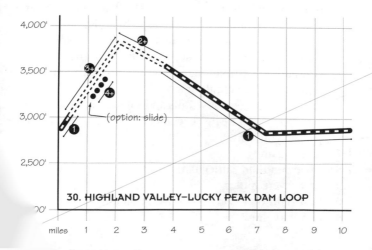

30. HIGHLAND VALLEY–LUCKY PEAK DAM LOOP

6.1 Lucky Peak Dam Observation Point is on your left. Dam road is also left just after this. Stay on Highway 21 down through a series of serious and sometimes congested curves. (Option: Go left onto dam road and then down gravel access road, to right and through gate just after crossing dam. This is a less intense route.)

7.2 Turn left off Highway 21 at Lucky Peak Lake sign. After turning off highway take an immediate right onto paved greenbelt (past wooden stile). Go left here on greenbelt to access Sandy Point Beach (swimming). The base of Lucky Peak Dam is visible just across the Boise River from here.

7.3 Cruise through Discovery State Park; this was originally the site of Foote House. Drinking water, restroom facilities, and lots of shade make this a great rest or lunch stop.

8.0 Following the Boise River Canyon, if you look up and to the right, you'll see one of the best local climbing areas in the basalt cliffs. The cliffs across the river and left are raptor habitat.

9.1 Diversion Dam is to left.

9.5 Pass under Highway 21 bridge.

10.1 Turn right off greenbelt. Go through cyclone fence/stile. Head up short, steep doubletrack hill to complete loop on Warm Springs Avenue.

Curlew Ridge Loop

Location: Boise Front, east of downtown Boise.

Distance: 6.8 miles.

Time: 1 to 2 hours.

Tread: Gravel road 1.2 miles; doubletrack 4.8 miles; singletrack 0.4 mile.

Aerobic level: Strenuous (the series of short steep climbs are sprints).

Technical difficulty: 1 to 3 on gravel; 2 to 5 on doubletrack.

Hazards: Traffic, shutter bumps, sandy spots on road; loose rock, short but severe steep climbs, and sand over rock on doubletrack. Suggestion: if you can't bike it up, do not bike it down.

Highlights: This loop starts at the botttom of Rocky Canyon, one of the most rugged and rocky places in Ada County. The approach just warms you up to the total pump of doing this ridge; views are direct into creeks some 500 feet below. The descent is a thrill; use caution.

Land status: Public. Access off the main road is restricted to specific uses in most places.

Maps: USGS Robie Creek, BLM Boise Front, Boise National rest, Ridge to Rivers.

ss: From downtown Boise at the northeast end, follow e Street north to Shaw Mountain Road. Follow Shaw

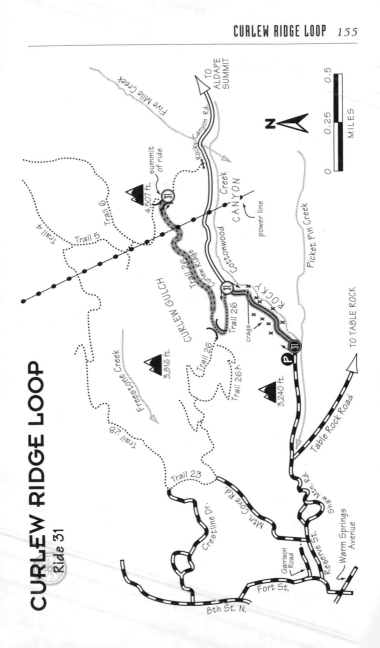

CURLEW RIDGE LOOP
Ride 31

Mountain Road to where it splits into Table Rock Road and
Rocky Canyon Road. Take Rocky Canyon Road (the left fork)
and follow it to the end of the pavement. There are extra paved
lanes here for staging and parking, but this is also used as a
turnaround spot, so park smart.

The Ride:

0.0 Starting on Rocky Canyon Road at the end of the pavement, pedal northeast up the main road. It is an easy to
moderate climb; watch out for traffic, blind turns, and
shutter bumps. Don't miss the crags, hoodoos, caves,
and balancing rocks that frame the lower canyon. You
can lunch and climb here.

0.6 Turn left off Rocky Canyon Road at a fast-rising
singletrack. It is marked with a Ridge to Rivers sign,
Trail 26. It was named Shane's Trail after the death of a

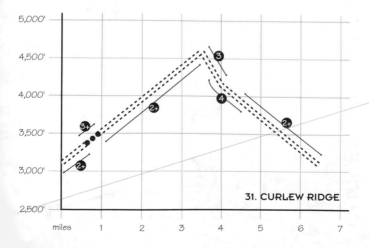

31. CURLEW RIDGE

local biker (he did not die biking). This new track switchbacks, dips, and climbs to a gentle ridge.

0.9 At ridgetop, bear right as trail becomes a doubletrack, drops, and then climbs fast. The trail gets rockier and trickier as you ascend.

1.4 Bear right (uphill) at ridgetop and climb another steep grade. There is an excellent view of Boise here, framed by buzzing towers.

1.7 Trail crests, dips, and eases.

2.0 Come down into a saddle with a steep entry and a soft bottom, then climb!

2.2 Trail crests; Rocky Canyon is to right (south), Curlew Gulch is left (north). Follow the undulating double-track as it rises and dips; mixed rock and sand toward the top of this section.

2.8 Rocky and soft trail continues up two more crests.

3.4 Come to a saddle with a steep hill just ahead. Go right (southeast) and down as you pass through open fence line. Doubletrack drops steeply at first and then follows an obvious line through wide open meadows. There are some very steep sections. Be content, for now, going back the way you came. The option of heading down into Rocky Canyon (going right here) may open up in the future.

6.8 Back at pavement.

Lower Curlew Ridge Loop

Location: Lower Boise foothills, east of downtown Boise.

Distance: 7.1 miles.

Time: 60 to 80 minutes.

Tread: 2.6 miles paved road, 1.2 miles gravel road, 0.2 miles doubletrack, 3.1 miles singletrack.

Aerobic level: Moderate.

Technical difficulty: 1 to 2 on gravel, 2 to 5 on singletrack.

Hazards: Traffic, shutter bumps, sandy spots, narrow trail in spots, some exposure.

Highlights: This varied and scenic ride starts and ends with cruising, rolling and curving pavement, takes you through the mouth of Rocky Canyon (a treat in itself), and for its main course, serves up a blend of benign to rigorous singletrack. It can be connected to Curlew Ridge proper or the Freestone Ridge trail to the west. It is close in, but you can feel far out!

Land status: Public access road. State, BLM land.

Maps: USGS Boise South, Boise North; Ridge to Rivers Trail System; BLM Boise Front.

Access: From downtown Boise at the northeast end, follow Reserve Street north to Shaw Mountain Road. Follow Shaw Mountain Road left to where it splits from Table Rock Road.

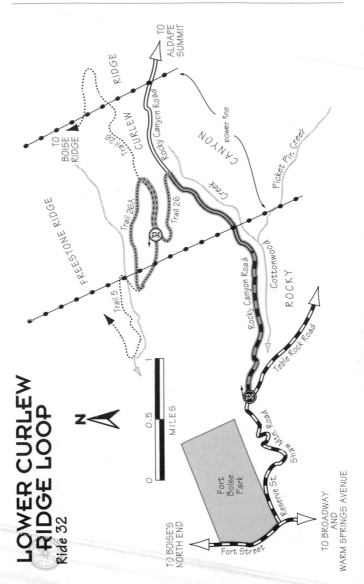

LOWER CURLEW
RIDGE LOOP
Ride 32

N

MILES
0   0.5   1

TO BOISE'S
NORTH END

Fort Boise Park

Reserve St.

Fort Street

TO BROADWAY
AND
WARM SPRINGS AVENUE

NE Mtn. Road

Table Rock Road

Rocky Canyon Road

ROCKY

Cottonwood

Creek

Picket Pin Creek

CANYON

power line

Rocky Canyon Road

Creek

Trail 26

Trail 26A

Trail 26

Trail 5

FREESTONE RIDGE

CURLEW   RIDGE

TO BOISE
RIDGE

TO
ALDAPE
SUMMIT

Shaw Mountain Road at this juncture (to the left) becomes Rocky Canyon Road. The ride starts here. There is limited parking available, but please be careful where and how you park; this is a residential area.

The Ride:

0.0 Start from the bottom of Rocky Canyon Road (where Table Rock Road splits from Shaw Mountain Road). This is a small crest, start easy, gliding cruise.

0.4 Cross cattleguards and dip as you cross Cottonwood Creek. Caution.

0.5 Begin winding and rolling climb up easy to moderate slope.

1.3 Pavement ends. Gravel road goes up steeper grade. Rocks and shutter bumps ensue.

1.6 This is the mouth of the canyon. Large rock crags tower

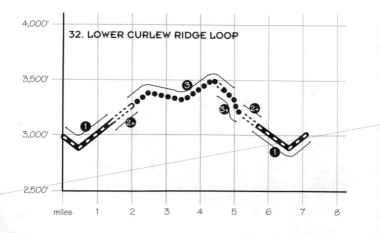

over the road. Some of the rocks are climbing quality, with the most striking formations jutting directly over Cottonwood Creek.

1.9 Go left up initially steep singletrack. This is a new Ridge to Rivers singletrack trail, Curlew Gulch/Ridge (Trail 26 in Ridge to Rivers), and which leads to the lower loop leg, Shane's Trail (Trail 26A). The start of this trail has a technical difficulty of 5 and, for most, a walk for the first 20 yards. After the hard start, this narrow sidehill trail has a couple of tricky dips. It's also exposed in some spots, so be prepared for oncoming bikers. Grade climbs moderately.

2.3 At saddle go right and down small dip. Views of Boise from this point on for the next couple of miles are superlative.

2.4 Go left at narrow singletrack (Trail 26A). Climb gentle sidehill.

2.5 Go down steep dip and over wooden bridge.

2.6 Grade flattens; trail follows contour.

3.2 Drop left down ridge, then join disintegrating doubletrack.

3.3 Down steep grade, trail is soft.

3.4 At fenceline go right and down.

3.5 Cross drainage bottom on single plank bridge. This is unique for this area, as far as I know.

3.6 Climb moderate to steep hill.

3.7 Gain ridge and bear right at fence line.

3.8 At trail T go right and up. Left will take you down into Curlew Gulch and up Freestone Ridge.

4.2 Gain ridgeline. Follow up right.

4.3 Gain crest and summit of this ride. Go right and down. Left leads up to Curlew Ridge itself.

4.6 Down steep doubletrack.

4.8 Rejoin trail by which you came, staying left. 26A is to right. Then climb short hill and bear left down new trail section by which you came.

5.1 Exposure on right and tricky dips.

5.2 Turn right at Rocky Canyon Road and return the way you came.

5.8 Rejoin pavement. Cruise in big ring.

6.6 Climb gently out of Cottonwood Creek.

7.1 Complete loop at crest.

Boise Ridge–Deer Point Loop

Location: Boise Front, just northwest of the center of town.

Distance: 25.3 miles.

Time: 3 to 4.5 hours.

Tread: 11.3 miles paved road; 7.6 miles dirt road; 6.4 miles doubletrack.

Aerobic level: Strenuous.

Technical difficulty: 1 to 4 on doubletrack; 1 to 2+ on dirt road; 1 to 2+ on pavement.

Hazards: Doubletrack has sand pockets, ruts, and loose rock; dirt road has ruts and water bars; pavement is patchy with some tight hairpins and poor visibility.

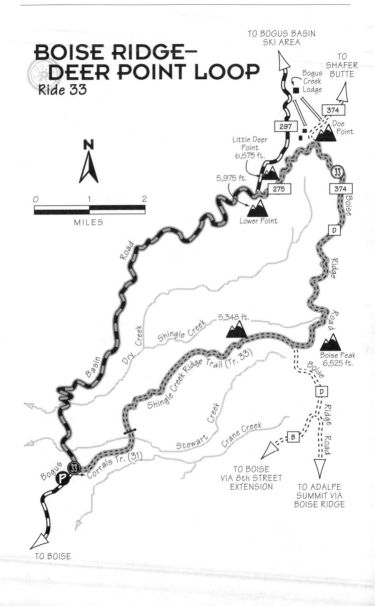

BOISE RIDGE—DEER POINT LOOP
Ride 33

TO BOGUS BASIN
SKI AREA

TO
SHAFER
BUTTE

Bogus
Creek
Lodge

374

297

Doe
Point

Little Deer
Point
6,575 ft.

33

5,975 ft.

275

374

Boise

Lower Point

D

N

Boise
Ridge
Road

0   1   2
MILES

Road

5,348 ft.

Boise Peak
6,525 ft.

Basin

Dry   Creek

Shingle Creek

Shingle Creek Ridge Trail (Tr. 33)

Boise
Ridge
Road

Stewart   Creek

Crane Creek

D

Bogus

33

P

Corrals Tr. (31)

B

TO BOISE
VIA 8th STREET
EXTENSION

TO ADALPE
SUMMIT VIA
BOISE RIDGE

TO BOISE

Highlights: This is a serious ride. Including the descents that you have to regain, this one climbs 4,000 feet. Terrain is widely varied, but the steep uphills are not so sustained or extreme in angle to make it cruel. Climbing to the Boise Ridge, you leave behind the semi-arid zone; pines, fir, and alders welcome you out of the sage. At the summit you have the option of climbing a bit more to plunge over the other side and down into Bogus Basin Ski Area.

Land status: Some of this ride is on private land; stay on marked trails only. The remainder is Boise National Forest, BLM and state land. Please obey the side trail closure signs; they are there to protect wildlife habitat.

Maps: Boise National Forest; USGS Boise North, Robie Creek, Shafer Butte; BLM Boise Front, Ridge to Rivers Trail System.

Access: From Boise's north end go 2.9 miles north on Bogus Basin Road from its intersection with Hill Road. There is a wide spot for parking half-a-dozen cars here. On the right (east) side of the road a wire gate defines the trailhead of a doubletrack which rises up an easy ridge. The ride starts here.

The Ride:

- **0.0** Follow soft doubletrack (Trail 31) through gate . Trail hugs gently inclined ridge.
- **1.0** Go through metal gate. Trail dips slightly.
- **1.4** Go left where doubletrack splits off toward metal gate. Go through gate and descend bumpy, hoof-beaten switchbacks. This is Trail 33, which, for the most part, ascends Shingle Creek Ridge.
- **1.8** Cross Stewart Creek. Stay on main doubletrack and begin climb.
- **1.9** Pass through metal gate; climb switchbacks.

2.6 Trail 33 marker indicates main trail bearing right. A doubletrack drops into the Dry Creek drainage, which is visible left. Grade eases.

2.7 Pass under power lines, then smooth gliding.

2.8 Steep push, follow undulating ridge.

3.0 Another push, but surface gets soft and sandy, mixed with loose rocks.

3.5 Gain ridge. Continue climbing mostly moderate now. For the next 0.5 mile a series of three crests and accompanying dips test your earnestness.

4.3 Go through a small saddle. Shingle Creek is now visible to the left (north), as is Shafer Butte (Bogus Basin) looking up. Climb rolling and steepening ridge to crest.

4.8 The doubletrack now repeats its favorite theme: a series of short, steep climbs with complementary glides.

5.4 Reach a stand of yellow pine. This is a great spot to smell the wonderful shade. Somehow the ride is more benign from this point on.

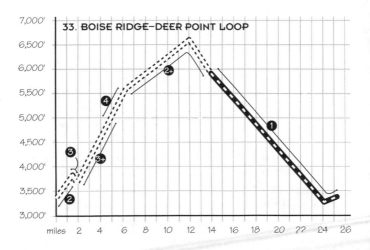

33. BOISE RIDGE—DEER POINT LOOP

5.6 Zoom small dip; get speed!

5.7 Climb steep; soft spots.

5.9 Steep again.

6.1 Reach crest amid firs. Shift into mid ring for a couple of gliding straightaways.

6.4 Go left (down) at Boise Ridge Road, which forks here. The ridge road is mostly smooth and firm, with occasional sandy spots (more toward the top) and ruts. Shady and cool under a canopy of mostly Douglas-fir, snow can lie in here until June.

6.6 Bottom out in dip.

6.7 Climb short and moderately steep hill. For the next mile the ridge road grade undulates and winds. Just about everything you descend, you reclimb, so have fun with this section.

7.6 Switchback gives way to smooth cruising.

8.0 Climb.

8.3 Cruise again.

8.5 Steep, short climb.

8.7 Grade eases, then flattens.

9.0 Resume climbing a steepening grade. This is one of the more serious tests of this ride.

9.5 Gain crest. View ahead (north skyline) is Deer Point (with communications towers). Descend briefly.

9.8 Climb a serious grade.

10.1 Large granite boulders and a hoodoo on left. Great view of large granite formations below Deer Point. The next 2 miles are a series of short, moderate-to-steep climbs with accompanying flats. Pace yourself.

12.0 Come to a Y junction. Metal gate to right has signs warning away motor vehicles; this road leads to the communications facilities and to Bogus Basin Ski Area. Go left down dirt road, which leads to Bogus Basin Road (old Boise Ridge Road). A sign there kindly informs you it is 18 miles back to town. This is the summit of this ride. You may be less than halfway through in total miles, but it's virtually one big descent from here. The elevation is 6,600 feet.

13.7 Logging road merges from left. Communications towers are visible ahead on Lower Point.

13.9 Bear right (down) at fork.

14.0 Come to Bogus Basin Road (paved). Turn left and down toward Boise. Watch for traffic, potholes, patches, and sand over pavement in spots. This is also a great time to zip up, as speeds exceeding 30 mph are possible on this road.

19.2 Pass through area with wonderful rock formations both sides of road.

20.7 Hairpin turn.

20.9 Pass under transmission lines.

22.5 Hairpin turns.

23.2 Go into hairpin and come out climbing moderate grade.

23.5 Reach crest and descend into straightaway.

23.7 Watch out for cattleguard.

23.9 Hairpin.

24.4 Grade flattens.

24.5 One more hairpin and then climb last hill to starting point and completion of loop at 25.3 miles. Now, turn around and do it the other way.

8th Street High Loop

Location: Boise Front, upper foothills northeast of downtown Boise.

Distance: 11.6 miles.

Time: 1.5 to 2.5 hours.

Tread: 6.4 miles on gravel/dirt road; 5.2 miles on singletrack.

Aerobic level: Strenuous.

Technical difficulty: 2 to 3 on roads; 2 to 5 on singletrack.

Hazards: All-terrain vehicle (ATV) traffic, soft and sandy pockets—sometimes enough to stop a runaway truck, sometimes sand over solid rock.

Highlights: This ride is an expressway to the Boise Ridge. Once on top, you're in expert territory (unless you've driven up), and the long rides of the area are at your pedals. This loop takes you back down as quickly as you came up. Do this ride without walking and you get the Iron Crotch Award. It takes skill, guts, and conditioning.

Land status: Public access roads and trails.

Maps: USGS Boise North, Robie Creek; Boise National Forest, BLM Boise Front, Ridge to Rivers Trail System.

Access: From downtown Boise go north on 8th Street. About 3 miles from the end of the pavement pull off to the right into the all-terrain vehicle parking lot. The ride starts from here.

8TH STREET HIGH LOOP
Ride 34

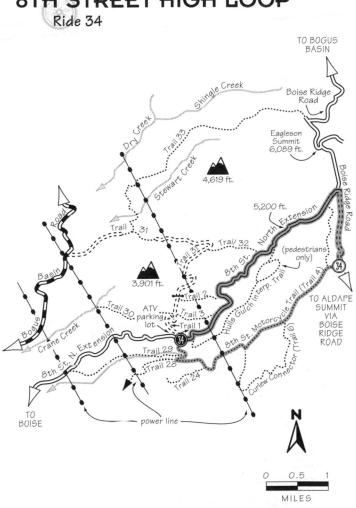

The Ride:

0.0 From the ATV parking lot on upper 8th Street pedal northeast (up) 8th Street. This route is well used and the surface changes at its own whim, so beware! Start climbing on sand, gravel, and rocks.

0.2 Hulls Gulch Interpretive Trail lower end trailhead on right.

0.8 First hill crest.

1.0 Reach a second, small crest.

1.2 Dip and climb!

2.2 Crest and glide a bit.

2.8 Grade becomes steep.

2.9 Pass bathroom facilities and the Hulls Gulch Interpretive Trail upper trailhead on right.

3.7 Steep and soft—surface offers marble- and softball-sized gravel on sand and rock.

4.0 Reach treeline, then steep pitch.

4.1 Crest and dip; you're surrounded by foliage as surface becomes smoother.

4.8 Go right (uphill) on Boise Ridge Road. It's marked as Trail D. Proceed up a series of smooth switchbacks. You are now under the summit canopy of trees.

5.1 Reach crest (and summit of this ride at 6,016 feet) on Boise Ridge.

5.7 Speed into dip.

5.8 Pump for crest and view right of Snake River Plain, Boise included.

5.9 Another dip, pump, and crest.

6.4 At small draw go right on singletrack, marked Trail 4. It cuts sidehill, and drops into a series of roots and rollers. Enjoy this tricky, but fun section. Difficulty 3+.

6.7 Come out of the trees. From shade to sun and sage, you're back in a semi-arid zone.

6.9   Go left down steep singletrack; this is the start of what is known as Devil's Slide. Difficulty goes to 4+. Compose yourself and be ready for the next 4 miles; it is sustained and requires a focused mind, but don't lose the big perspective here. You could probably launch your hanglider from a dozen spots; the worst launch is over your handlebars. Walking your bike in spots is an option.

7.3   Soft. Down slightly and standup rollers.

7.6   Soft, dip, then climb gently.

7.8   At small rise turn right to sidehill trail down. Trail 6 goes left here.

7.9   Steep, loose rocks, and sandy.

8.1   Grade flattens.

8.2   Drop steeply again. Take a moment, though. From here you can see just about every major trail in the Boise Front. This spot may be the center of it all. Trail becomes soft and rocky.

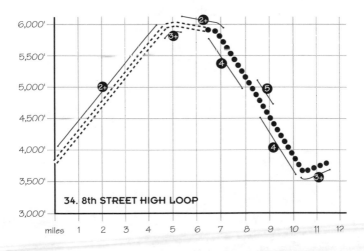

34. 8th STREET HIGH LOOP

8.4 Trail mellows briefly, then goes steep, soft, and rocky (again).

8.6 Some exposure on right (not sheer, but good tumble potential).

8.7 Difficulty approaches 5; bedrock, sand, and loose rocks.

8.8 Grade mellows, but deep sand (wheels go sideways).

9.0 Trail 6 junction to left. Bear right and down, continuing on Trail 4.

9.5 Steep and rocky as you pass under power line.

9.7 Steep sidehill; soft and rocky.

10.1 Negotiate hairpin and climb.

10.2 Gain saddle. Trail 24 (Sidewinder) junction is to left. Stay right and continue down Trail 4. 8th Street ATV lot is directly west and visible from here on the next ridge over.

10.7 Hairpin and quick up.

10.8 Go right at trail junction and up slightly. Trail 28, the Crestline Trail, is to the left.

11.0 Cross creek and go right up a series of switchbacks; grade gets serious in spots.

11.6 Enter ATV lot through fenceline. Bear right to complete loop.

Shingle Creek Ridge Loop

Location: Boise Front, just northwest of the center of town.

Distance: 14.4 miles.

Time: 2 to 3.5 hours.

Tread: 13 miles of doubletrack;1.4 miles of singletrack.

Aerobic level: Strenuous.

Technical difficulty: 1 to 4+ on doubletrack; 2 to 4 on singletrack.

Hazards: Doubletrack has sand pockets, sand over rock, ruts, loose rock; singletrack has narrow, exposed, and rocky sections with tight sagebrush passages. All-terrain vehicles on the Boise Ridge Road and 8th Street.

Highlights: This is one of the more serious classics of the Boise Front. Terrain is widely varied, and the steep uphills are not so sustained or extreme in angle to make it a "pig grunt." Climbing to the Boise Ridge, you leave behind the ubiquitous sage and cheatgrass; yellow pines, Douglas-fir, and aspen make it seem you are in a sub-alpine zone.

Land status: Some of this ride is on private land; stay on marked trails only. The remainder is BLM and state land. Please obey the side trail closure signs; they are there to protect wild-life habitat.

SHINGLE CREEK RIDGE LOOP
Ride 35

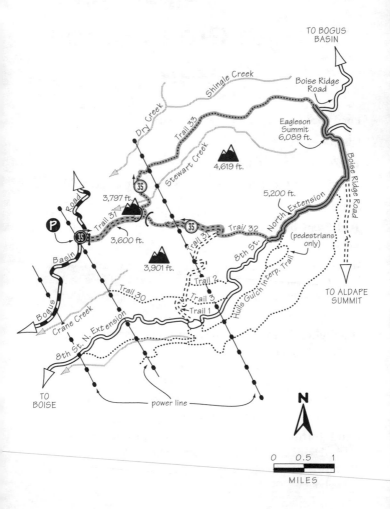

TO BOGUS BASIN

Boise Ridge Road

Shingle Creek

Dry Creek

Trail 33

Eagleson Summit 6,089 ft.

Stewart Creek

4,619 ft.

Boise Ridge Road

P

Road

3,797 ft.

35

Trail 31

3,600 ft.

35

Trail 31

5,200 ft.

North Extension

Trail 32

(pedestrians only)

8th St.

3,901 ft.

Basin

Trail 2

Trail 3

Trail 1

Hulls Gulch Interp. Trail

TO ALDAPE SUMMIT

Trail 30

Bogus

Crane Creek

8th St. N. Extension

TO BOISE

power line

N

0   0.5   1

MILES

Maps: Boise National Forest, USGS Boise North, BLM Boise Front, Ridge to Rivers.

Access: From Boise's North End go 2.9 miles north on Bogus Basin Road from its intersection with Hill Road. There is a wide spot for parking half-a-dozen cars here. On the right (east) side of the road a wire gate defines the trailhead of a doubletrack which rises up an easy ridge. The ride starts here.

The Ride:

0.0   Follow soft doubletrack through gate; this is Trail 31 (Corrals). Trail hugs gently inclined ridge.
1.0   Go through metal gate. Trail dips slightly.
1.4   Go left where doubletrack splits off toward metal gate. Go through gate and descend bumpy switchbacks. This is Trail 33 (Shingle Creek Ridge Trail).
1.8   Cross Stewart Creek. Stay on main doubletrack, and begin climb.
1.9   Pass through metal gate; climb switchbacks.
2.6   Trail 33 marker indicates main trail bearing right. A doubletrack drops into the Dry Creek drainage, which is visible to the left. Grade eases.
2.7   Pass under power lines, then smooth gliding.
2.8   Steep push; follow undulating ridge.
3.0   Another push, but surface gets soft and sandy, mixed with loose rocks.
3.5   Gain ridge. Continue climbing moderately now. For the next half mile, a series of three crests and accompanying dips test your earnestness.
4.3   Go through a small saddle. Shingle Creek is now visible to the left (north), as is Shafer Butte looking up. Climb rolling and steepening ridge to crest.

4.8 Bear left to stay on Trail 33. (Going right on rocky doubletrack leads down a series of three ridgetops and then plunges into Stewart Creek drainage to where we first crossed it.) Doubletrack now repeats its favorite theme: a series of short steep climbs with complementary glides.

5.4 Reach a stand of yellow pine.

5.6 Zoom small dip; get speed!

5.7 Climb steep grade with soft spots.

5.9 Steep again.

6.1 Reach crest amid firs. Shift into mid ring for a couple of gliding straightaways.

6.4 Go right (up) road fork (Boise Ridge Road). The ridge road climbs moderately as it winds around the west side. Shady and cool under a canopy of mostly Douglas-fir, snow can lie in here until June.

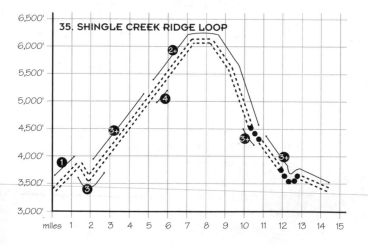

7.3   Eagleson Summit. Road signs list the various mileages. Bear right and down. Watch for heavy rutting and traffic.

8.0   Glide through area of private dwellings.

8.2   At 3-way fork bear right and down.

8.4   At junction of trails B and D, go right on B. This is the top of 8th Street. As you follow it down, be aware, it is mostly rock and sand, and some places fine powder.

9.1   Caution! This is a rocky, steep, and rutted section.

9.3   Most of the Boise Valley is in view from here, but it is kind of small. Soft sections ahead.

10.2   Hulls Gulch Interpretive Trail is marked on the left (pedestrians only). There are restroom facilities here.

10.3   Turn right off 8th Street onto Trail 32 (Scott's Trail). After going over a bar gate, it is a narrow singletrack that drops easily, but is exposed in places. Sagebrush is close and sharp in here and can hide some little rock surprises.

11.3   At draw, terrain and trail ease, open up.

11.4   Make a sharp right on Trail 31 (probably unmarked), which descends into Crane Creek drainage. Ruts and loose rocks contribute to the trickiness of this downhill section. At times it's hard to tell if it is 1 track or 2.

12.4   Cross Crane Creek. Weathered granite outcroppings to your side and power lines above.

12.5   Pass through metal gate. Pulverized granite makes for a smooth ride in here.

12.6   Climb out of Crane Creek Canyon on singletrack.

12.9   Trail turns to doubletrack as you enter saddle.

13.0   Trail 33 and gate (the way we came) are to the right at a fork. Stay left on main trail.

13.4   Go through metal gate.

14.2   Pass under power lines.

14.4   Come to wire gate (Trailhead 31) and Bogus Basin Road to complete loop.

Shafer Butte Loop

Location: Upper Boise Front Range, Bogus Basin Ski Area.

Distance: 12.8 miles.

Time: 2 to 3 hours.

Tread: 2.4 miles on pavement; 10.4 miles doubletrack/dirt road.

Aerobic level: Moderate to strenuous.

Technical difficulty: 1 on pavement; 1 to 3 off pavement.

Hazards: Soft pockets, fixed/loose rock, traffic on Deer Point and Bogus Basin roads.

Highlights: This ride takes you to the summit of the Boise Ridge. It gives you a good chance to see Bogus Basin, which is almost alpine, in the summer. Once you get up to the top (Shafer Butte), there are dozens of possiblities for thrill rides; knowing the ski area helps.

Land status: Public, Boise National Forest.

Maps: Boise National Forest; USGS Shafer Butte.

Access: From Boise's North End, starting your odometer from the intersection of Bogus Basin and Hill roads, drive 14.2 miles up Bogus Basin Road. Turn right onto Deer Point Road), which is presently unmarked except for a single steel pole next to double wooden posts. Go up a short, steep hill and park at either of a couple of shaded pullouts just uphill of the initial fork.

SHAFER BUTTE LOOP
Ride 36

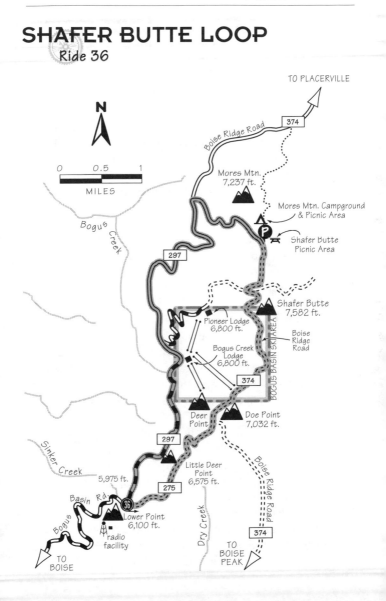

TO PLACERVILLE

Boise Ridge Road

374

N

0   0.5   1
MILES

Mores Mtn.
7,237 ft.

Mores Mtn. Campground
& Picnic Area

Shafer Butte
Picnic Area

Bogus Creek

297

Shafer Butte
7,582 ft.

Pioneer Lodge
6,800 ft.

Boise
Ridge
Road

Bogus Creek
Lodge
6,800 ft.

BOGUS BASIN SKI AREA

374

Deer
Point

Doe Point
7,032 ft.

297

Sinker Creek

Little Deer
Point
6,575 ft.

5,975 ft.

Boise Ridge Road

Basin Rd.

275

36

Bogus

Lower Point
6,100 ft.

radio
facility

Dry Creek

374

TO
BOISE

TO
BOISE PEAK

The ride (and mileage) starts from where this dirt road meets Bogus Basin Road.

The Ride:

0.0 From the junction of Deer Point (FR 275) and Bogus Basin (FR 297) roads pedal up (northeast) Deer Point Road. It is well used and mostly smooth; be aware, it is not just all-terrain vehicles that come whipping along here. Sand pockets in spots contribute to the grudge of the grade.

0.2 Grade eases.

0.3 Stay left on main track. Grade becomes moderate.

1.2 Deer Point communications facilities come into view straight ahead.

1.3 Grade steepens. Granite hoodoos and dome faces are all around here; don't miss the bliss because your ticker feels thicker.

2.0 Deer Point Road ends as it Ts into Boise Ridge Road (FR 374) here. Go left through a metal boom gate and up a steep, rocky section. You're now on the old Boise Ridge Road, and a century ago, this was the way to Idaho City from Boise. Big, beautiful firs are here just for you to stop and pant under.

2.1 Bear right as you reach the base of the communication towers.

2.2 Reach crest, then go right (up) at 3-way split, bearing just left of the Deer Point Chairlift top.

2.3 Go left on doubletrack, staying to top of ridge.

2.5 Pass under Showcase Chairlift and continue down ridge and ill-defined track. Views stretch east to the Sawtooths and across the Boise Range.

2.6 Meet lower ridge road and bear right.

2.7 Pump through dip and start the climb for Shafer Butte itself. The trail on the right leads to Pine Creek and the backside of the mountain; stay left. Grade gets serious.

3.2 Bear left and stay to main track. Upper Nugget ski run is to right.

3.4 Round curve and come to a great vantage of Bogus Basin itself. This was a goldfield long before anybody thought of skiing (or biking) here. Grade eases.

3.6 Climb moderate grade.

4.1 Reach Shafer Butte saddle. Top of Superior Chair is to left, and Shafer Butte summit trail is to right. Take middle-doubletrack, which goes right and down. Keep to the main trail (still FR 374) which descends for the 1.5 miles in a series of switchbacks. This part is a lot of fun; Kelly humps, logs, rocks, and ruts always seem to return to a relatively smooth track. Difficulty goes to 3 in places.

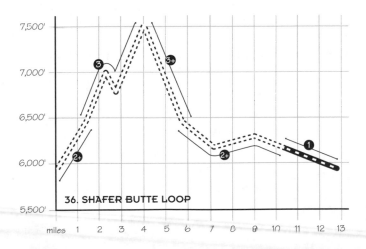

36. SHAFER BUTTE LOOP

5.6 Come to bottom of grade and ski area boundary warning sign. Bear right (up) at the fork. You are now in the saddle between Shafer Butte and Mores Mountain.

5.7 Go around metal gate, bearing left.

5.8 At pavement (FR 366) go left. Just to the right is the Shafer Butte Picnic Area (hence, the pavement). Water and restroom facilities are available there.

5.9 To right is the Mores Mountain campground/picnic site; the trailhead to the Mores Mountain loop trail is also there. Stay left when the brief patch of paved Nirvana turns back to Idaho standard gravel and dirt. Descend.

7.1 Go left onto FR 297 at its junction with FR 374. Watch for rocky, washboard sections.

7.9 Bottom of grade; begin climb.

8.9 Grade crests and levels.

10.0 Pass nordic trailhead hut and potties on right. Bear right and level to main road. Riding stables and Pioneer Lodge Road (paved) are up and to the left here.

10.4 Go through Bogus Basin Ski Area main parking lot.

10.5 Pavement begins.

10.9 Climb gentle hill.

11.0 Grade flattens.

12.0 Begin cruising glide.

12.8 Come to Deer Point Road and completion of loop.

Lower Nordic Loop

Location: Bogus Basin Ski Area, 16 miles north of Boise.

Distance: 4.1 miles.

Time: 30 to 60 minutes.

Tread: 3.5 miles of doubletrack; 0.6 mile of dirt/gravel road.

Aerobic level: Easy.

Technical difficulty: 1 to 3+ on doubletrack; 1 to 2 on road.

Hazards: Sand pockets, rocks, ruts, and a few short steep grades; traffic on road.

Highlights: This ride follows the Bogus Basin Lower Nordic Loop trails. It's full of changes: saddles, crests, dips, and rollers. Steeps are not sustained, and obstacles are moderate at worst. Best of all, if you have a mind to explore and do not mind an occasional backtrack, there are many creative options.

Land status: Boise National Forest and Bogus Basin Ski Area.

Maps: USGS Shafer Butte, Boise National Forest, Bogus Nordic Trail Map.

Access: From Boise's North End (at the intersection of Hill and Bogus Basin roads), travel up Bogus Basin Road, north about 16.5 miles. When the pavement ends, you will see the lower (main) parking lot near the Bogus Creek Lodge. The trail starts just beyond the Nordic Hut, at the Nordic Trailhead, about 0.3 mile past the main parking lot.

LOWER NORDIC LOOP
Ride 37

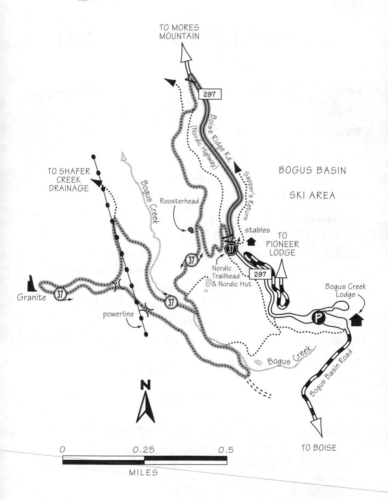

TO MORES
MOUNTAIN

297

Boise Ridge Rd.
(Nordic Highway)

Sapper's Return

BOGUS BASIN

SKI AREA

TO SHAFER
CREEK
DRAINAGE

Bogus Creek

Roosterhead

stables

TO
PIONEER
LODGE

37   37

Nordic
Trailhead
& Nordic Hut

297

Bogus Creek
Lodge

Granite   37

P

powerline

37

Bogus Creek

Bogus Basin Road

N

TO BOISE

0   0.25   0.5

MILES

The Ride:

0.0 From the Nordic Trailhead on Bogus Basin Road (FR 297), called the Nordic Highway in winter, pedal north. It is mostly flat and smooth.

0.6 Make a sharp left onto a doubletrack which descends gently down a sidehill. Go around a steel gate and into the trees.

0.8 Downgrade steepens and surface gets bumpy.

0.9 Enter granite boulder area.

1.2 Meet main Nordic Trail loop. Go right, descending gently on doubletrack just left of a large granite roosterhead.

1.5 Ride through open meadow with slide alders crowding Bogus Creek bottom. Bear right on doubletrack that crosses creek. The bumpy track smooths somewhat after the creek and becomes a fun cruiser.

1.8 Bottom out and begin easy climb.

1.9 Pedal up to saddle, bearing left as you pass under power lines, past large granite hoodoos on your right. Doubletrack rises gently as it follows power lines.

2.0 Begin climbing the first of two short, but moderately steep hills, the second of which is more sustained.

2.2 Gain crest and then curve right on main trail, which drops quickly to a small saddle. Another drop rockets you through a draw and a short, smooth cruise.

2.3 Bear left at fork and up gentle rise.

2.4 A granite prominence on your right defines the ridgetop you have reached here. Bear left and head up ridge.

2.5 Swoop and climb through a set of double dips.

2.7 Bear right at a doubletrack fork in a small saddle.

2.8 Drop into a deeper saddle (soft and rocky) and start climbing.

2.9 Climb another short steep.

3.0 Crest and glide on a soft rolling trail.

3.1 Bear left and down at split.

3.2 Enter Bogus Creek bottom again; cross the creek at a switchback with big alders. Stay left along creek bottom.

3.4 Pass small outbuilding and continue up the main trail on the right side of the meadow. To your left is the trail you looped in on. Climb up main trail, ignoring the two steep rights.

3.7 Go right, up a sandy switchback, past the granite roosterhead. Climb through a series of soft, moderately steep curves. Bear right through this section.

3.9 Merge left onto a larger sidehill trail, climbing on soft and rocky ground.

4.0 Go up a right-leading switchback (this is a bit tricky, maintaining uphill speed and balance on the soft trail), and then through a metal gate.

4.1 Return to road at Nordic Trailhead and complete loop.

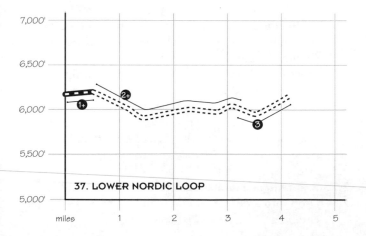

37. LOWER NORDIC LOOP

Elk Meadows

Location: Bogus Basin Ski Area, 19 miles north of Boise.

Distance: 4.1 miles.

Time: 30 to 60 minutes.

Tread: 0.8 mile of singletrack; 3.3 miles of doubletrack/ski access-road.

Aerobic level: Easy to moderate.

Technical difficulty: 2 to 4 on singletrack; 1 to 3 on doubletrack.

Hazards: Soft pockets, rocks, boulders, water bars, and narrow sidehill with some exposure. Expect exposure to wind and chilly temperatures; a light shell may be appropriate even on summer days.

Highlights: Circumnavigating the top of Shafer Butte, this ride is the highest in this book.

Land status: Boise National Forest and Bogus Basin Ski Area.

Maps: USGS Shafer Butte, Boise National Forest; Bogus Basin Ski Area Trail Map.

Access: From Boise's North End (at the intersection of Hill and Bogus Basin roads), travel north up Bogus Basin Road about 16.5 miles. The pavement ends at the lower (main) parking lot near the Bogus Creek Lodge. Proceed on the Boise Ridge Road (which continues through the main parking lot) to 16.9 miles, where the sandy surface turns to pavement as it leaves the main

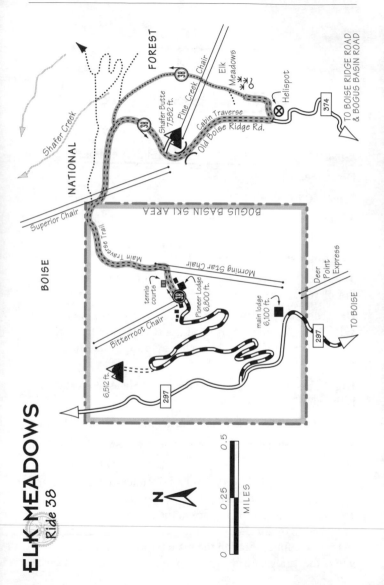

ELK MEADOWS
Ride 38

ridge road and splits right, up through a series of switchbacks to the Pioneer Lodge. Park at the lodge; mileage starts from here.

The Ride:

0.0 From the Pioneer Lodge parking lot, directly in front of the lodge, pedal east and up behind the lodge.

0.1 Pass tennis courts on your left as the doubletrack becomes more defined. The trail climbs a short, steep hill under Morningstar Chairlift and S-curves up to the right of the lift shack and bullwheel at the top.

0.2 Get on the main traverse trail to access the Superior and Pine Creek sides of the ski area. Nightskiing lights (Bogus has one of the most extensive nightskiing operations in the country) lead the way. For the next 0.5 mile, four short, moderate hills punctuate the gradual rise.

0.8 Come to an open ski run and a fork in the trail. Go right and continue climbing. Watch out for a thin section of eroded trail here. Mores Mountain is visible, just to the north.

1.0 Doubletrack splits here (with a steep singletrack in between); go right and up switchback. Climb through a soft steep section.

1.2 Pedal up a switchback, to the right (Majestic Run and Superior Chair access signs, on your left).

1.3 Climb through a soft and steep section.

1.5 Bear left and up at the saddle. This is the summit of this ride. To the right is the top of the Superior Chair, and to the left is the top of Shafer Butte (you can't miss it with all the communications towers). Continue straight ahead and over the saddle; this is now the Cabin

Traverse ski trail, named for an old miner's hut from the local gold rush. Descend moderately on a firm road, but beware of the pulverized granite on the bedrock surface.

2.0 Turn left, off of the Cabin Traverse, to join the Upper Nugget Trail—a grassy, bumpy, ill-defined doubletrack with water bars.

2.1 Take a sharp, soft left (this is the main Nugget trail) onto a doubletrack that goes sidehill through an open meadow. The summit of Shafer Butte is above and behind you.

2.2 There is a spring is to the right as the trail narrows to singletrack and contours out of the meadow.

2.3 Narrow trail (4+) and increasing obstacles make sections in the next 0.5 mile the most technical of this ride. This is an especially fun section with short, winding steep sections; boulders; and an intermittent canopy of giant firs. As you descend slightly, speed and momentum can be used to mitigate the delicate upswings.

2.4 Crest, and merge with a singletrack on your left. Diffi-

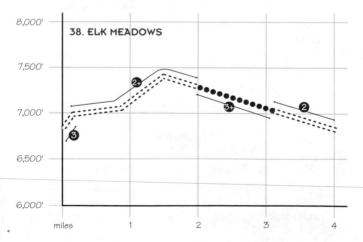

culty eases as you bear right and sidehill through a rolling meadow.

2.6 Roll over the plateau, past a line of large firs on your right.

2.7 Pass under the Pine Creek Chairlift. Obstacles increase and difficulty ebbs to 3+. There is a good view to the east from here of the Boise Range and the Sawtooth Mountains.

2.8 Begin dropping again as obstacles increase.

2.9 Exercise caution here. The sidehill angle increases, there is some exposure, and the trail is very soft and narrow in places. Technical difficulty 4.

3.0 Merge with doubletrack (Paradise access road) and bear left.

3.1 At fork, go left and climb uphill.

3.3 At the Superior Chairlift, take the left fork (where you came in).

3.4 Pass beneath the Superior Chairlift and you are back on the main traverse road, headed back to the Pioneer Lodge. Mostly smooth cruising.

3.9 At the top of the Morningstar Chairlift, bear right, around the towers, and head down.

4.0 A short, steep hill under the chair will shoot you past the tennis courts. Take either fork around Pioneer Lodge to complete the loop.

Mores Mountain Loop

Location: Upper Boise Front Range, north of Bogus Basin Ski Area.

Distance: 4.6 miles.

Time: 30 to 60 minutes.

Tread: 3.1 miles doubletrack/dirt road; 1.5 miles singletrack.

Aerobic level: Easy to moderate.

Technical difficulty: 2 to 3 on doubletrack/dirt road; 2 to 5 on singletrack.

Hazards: Soft pockets, fixed/loose rock, and Kelly humps; traffic on roads.

Highlights: Mores Mountain is one of the few peaks in the Boise Range that rises above 7,000 feet in elevation. The summit of this ride is about 6,600 feet, but the pedestrian-only nature loop will take you to the top. There are beautiful, high lupine meadows near the summit and some interesting rock crags (climbing-quality, even). The steep, singletrack section of this ride is a wonderful mix of rocks, humps, and granitic sand. If you ride from the other direction, the difficult crux sections are half as difficult. There are at least a half-dozen granite spires that greet you along this trail, not counting the domes, hoodoos, and buttresses that surprise you along the way. It is a short sprint, so if you are going to drive all that way to get there (many sprocketheads will pedal the approach) you might as well take advantage of one of the area's many available tangents.

Land status: Public, Boise National Forest.

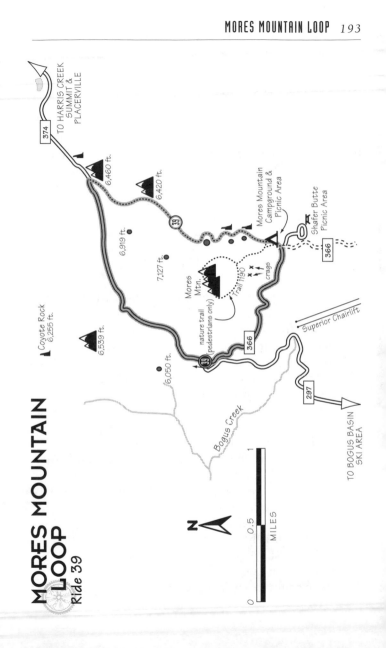

MORES MOUNTAIN LOOP
Ride 39

N

0   0.5   1
MILES

TO HARRIS CREEK
SUMMIT &
PLACERVILLE

374

6,460 ft.

6,420 ft.

39

Mores Mountain
Campground &
Picnic Area

Shafer Butte
Picnic Area

366

6,919 ft.

7,127 ft.

Mores
Mtn.

Trail 1190

crags

nature trail
(pedestrians only)

Coyote Rock
6,255 ft.

6,539 ft.

366

Superior Chairlift

39

6,050 ft.

297

TO BOGUS BASIN
SKI AREA

Bogus Creek

Maps: Boise National Forest; USGS Shafer Butte.

Access: From Boise's North End, start your odometer at the intersection of Bogus Basin and Hill roads, and drive 16.5 miles north, up Bogus Basin Road. Staying to the left, drive through the parking lot on a sandy dirt road. At 17 miles, bear left on the Bogus Basin Road, go between two red steel posts and pass the Nordic Trailhead hut. Continue on this road (FR 297) for another 2.9 miles, to where the Shafer Butte Picnic Area Road and the Boise Ridge Road meet. Park here; there are ample shoulders. The ride starts here.

The Ride:

0.0   From the junction of FR 297 and Shafer Butte Picnic Area (FR 366) roads, pedal north on FR 297. The road is mostly smooth, with occasional soft pockets and loose rock. It is a moderate climb around the NW side of Mores Mountain.

0.6   For the next few tenths of a mile, check out the interesting granite formations to your left.

1.0   At a small crest, go around a cattleguard and descend.

1.4   Coyote Rock, an almost-spire with an impressive face and crown is on your left. The road levels out.

1.7   Go right at a singletrack that takes off sharply up a Kelly hump. Shift into low ring; this is the start of the real ride. Climb over a series of humps with mostly smooth surfaces. Difficulty is 4+.

1.9   Grade eases briefly.

2.0   Descend briefly.

2.1   Climb past a granite dome, to the right. The trail becomes rocky and soft.

2.3   Twin spires to left (east). Continue moderate climb.

2.4 Difficulty approaches 5 as the soft and rocky trail winds through domes and spires. Water bars add to challenge. Keep climbing.

2.5 Grade and difficulty ease; trail smooths out.

2.7 Small crest and dip.

2.8 The difficulty eases here, to 3+, but the trail gets rocky and rolls up and down.

2.9 Granite spires to left, domes to right. Continue climbing.

3.1 Go left when the singletrack forks; a gentle downhill. This is the edge of the nature-trail meadow.

3.2 Singletrack merges with the doubletrack leading to the nature- trailhead/approach. Leave your bike and go right at the dirt road, if you want to hike the Mores Mountain summit loop. This is the Mores Mountain Camp and Picnic Area.

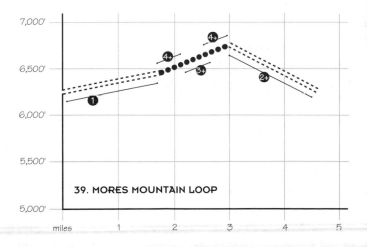

39. MORES MOUNTAIN LOOP

3.3 Go right (down) on gravel road (unmarked FR 366) . Watch out for invisible shutter bumps on this road; they'll shake you off your frame if you are not careful. You have completed the loop when you arrive back at FR 297.

Sappers Return Loop

Location: Bogus Basin Ski Area, 16 miles north of Boise.

Distance: 4.8 miles.

Time: 45 to 60 minutes.

Tread: 2.6 miles of doubletrack; 2.1 miles of dirt/gravel road; 0.2 mile of singletrack.

Aerobic level: Easy.

Technical difficulty: 3 to 4+ on singletrack; 2 to 4 on doubletrack.

Hazards: Sand pockets, rocks, ruts and a few steep sections; traffic on road.

Highlights: This loop is mostly through a canopy of trees. It is all above 6,000 feet elevation. It follows the Nordic trail system at Bogus; its turnaround point is at the lower end of the Superior Chairlift. The loop is full of changes and not heavily used.

Land status: Boise National Forest and Bogus Basin Ski Area.

Maps: USGS Shafer Butte, Boise National Forest, Bogus Basin Ski Area Nordic Map.

SAPPERS RETURN LOOP
Ride 40

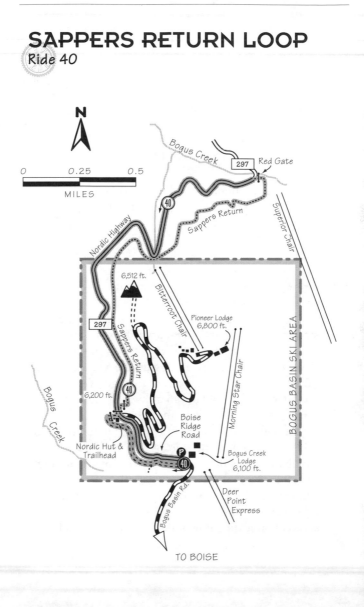

N

| 0 | 0.25 | 0.5 |

MILES

Bogus Creek

297 Red Gate

40

Sappers Return

Superior Chair

Nordic Highway

6,512 ft.

Bitterroot Chair

Pioneer Lodge
6,800 ft.

297

Sappers Return

40

6,200 ft.

Morning Star Chair

BOGUS BASIN SKI AREA

Bogus Creek

Boise
Ridge
Road

Nordic Hut &
Trailhead

P
40

Bogus Creek
Lodge
6,100 ft.

Deer
Point
Express

Bogus Basin Rd.

TO BOISE

Access: From Boise's north end (at the intersection of Hill and Bogus Basin Roads), travel up Bogus Basin Road north about 16.5 miles. When the pavement ends, you're at the lower (main) parking lot near the Bogus Creek Lodge. The trail starts just below the parking and to the left (southwest) as you drive in. It's a new trail at this point, so it may be a bit soft at first.

The Ride:

0.0 Take the new doubletrack that plunges down southwest of the lower, main parking lot. After the initial 20-foot drop, the trail heads west on a sidehill, following the main Bogus Basin Road (FR 297), which leads through the parking lot. Track is sandy and rocky, a theme that holds true for most of this ride.

0.1 Bear right at forks that drop left and down; continue on contour and up slightly.

0.5 Come over small rise, dip, and climb moderate, short, steep section through an S-curve. This is a great picnic site, complete with natural granite sculpture.

0.6 Walk around metal gate and gain the Ridge Road (still FR 297). Nordic shack is just to the right. Go left briefly on Ridge Road, then take an immediate right and climb the dirt road that leads to the riding stables.

0.7 Go through metal gate and then take an immediate left; this doubletrack is the start of Sappers Return.

0.8 Climb through small crests. Soft sand makes it tougher than it looks.

1.3 Climb small hill to a northwesterly vista. Bogus Creek drainage is to the west; Stack Rock is to the south. A series of large dips now follow. Delicate speed helps.

1.7 Leave trees momentarily and enter the slide area, descending to the bottom of Morning Star Chairlift. Go right and pass the lift shack.

1.8 Trail narrows as it winds left through meadow.

1.9 Trail briefly turns to singletrack (4) as it climbs the hill of this ride; it is steep and soft. If you can stay on your bike here, you are in shape.

2.0 Crest this hill and wind into trees.

2.1 Doubletrack resumes; reach saddle and multi-forks in large Douglas-fir stand. Remains of a fire camp is on left. Take second trail from right and plunge down. The granite crags of Mores Mountain are visible above the route.

2.3 Join a descending ski trail; follow the night lights. Continue down rutted, steep slope.

2.4 Go right on singletrack where it splits around copse, eases grade and drops again.

2.5 Bear left just above bottom of Superior Chairlift.

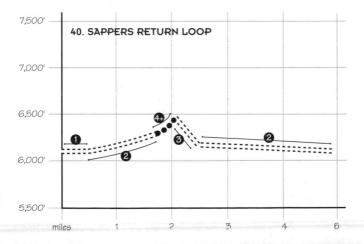

2.6 Go through metal boom gate and bear left at the Boise Ridge Road. Climb mostly smooth, sandy surface.

2.7 Grade steepens, shutter bumps.

3.0 Grade eases.

3.5 Grade flattens.

3.7 Grade climbs slightly.

4.3 Pass Nordic hut, staying on main road. Follow flat road back to main parking lot and complete loop.

Appendix A

Other Boise-area Routes

Here is a short listing, with brief descriptions, of other roads and trails in the Boise area. These are routes that offer rides of marginal quality; remember, this is a **mountain** biking guide. For one reason or another, they were not included in the main selection. They make good alternatives when your favorite trails are full of crowds, mud, or snow.

Hulls Traverse - From Camelback Park in the North End go north on a wide, sandy singletrack, following the east side of Camelback Ridge itself. Do not cross the creek; just hug the dromedarian feature, staying in the flats and off the ridge. This leads to a gravel service road and water tank. Follow the road east to 8th Street (just after a metal gate). Go either left (up) or right (down) 8th Street to any number of trails. Heading up, across, and then right, will take you to the gulch proper. Heading down and then going left after 0.1 mile, off of 8th Street, will take you across the creek, which leads to Hulls Grove and a few trails on its eastern edge.

Freestone Ridge - Designated Trail 5 in the Ridge to Rivers System, this steep grunt (or plunge, depending on which way you do it) can be accessed from the bottom end via Ridge to Rivers Trail 26 (see Ride 32 of this book) or from the top via Ridge to Rivers Trails 4 and 6 (see Ride 31 of this book).

Boise Ridge Road - Designated Trail D in the Ridge to Rivers System, this four-wheel-drive road takes off north from Aldape Summit. A grueling series of switchbacks and steep climbs, this route connects to 8th Street, Eagleson Summit, and Bogus Basin. Once you are on top of the ridge itself, it is more benign and offers a variety of possibilities. Views are superlative, but beware, the ride is mostly above 5,000 feet, and you're not close in, so be prepared.

Upper Squaw Creek Ridge Trail - This northern section of Ridge to Rivers Trail 8 is accessed from the bottom via Ridge to Rivers Trails 12 or 13 (see Ride 29 of this book) or from the top via Shaw Mountain Road (see Ride 13 of this book). This is a real hill climb or plunge with demanding switchbacks but incredible views.

The **World Center for Birds of Prey** is located about 7 miles south of Boise; just follow Cole Road south. A sign directs you off the main road right and up a smooth, steep hill. The center offers viewing, information, and opportunities to support this unique and worthy facility. Cloverdale Road, from Boise, through Kuna and then south, will lead you to the Snake River Birds of Prey National Conservation Area; an information stop is just south of Kuna. At this area, along the northern rim of the Snake River Canyon, a 10-mile section of multi-use trail (non-motorized) stretches between Swan Falls Dam to Celebration Park. If you're a birder or nature-lover, these places are a must see.

Other places close to Boise offer a wide range of rides. Idaho City, northeast of town on Highway 21, is fast becoming a mountain biking mecca, especially after the 8th Street fire in Boise closed a number of Central Front trails. Warm Springs Point Road, Slaughterhouse Gulch, and Pine Creek Roads are good starting points. The South and Middle Forks of the Payette River offer an incredible range of scenery and terrain. Only an hour's drive from town (north, up Highways 55 or 21), these drainages present some of the best whitewater and geothermal dipping opportunities in the West. Trails abound out of Garden Valley, Deadwood Gulch, and north of Hardscrabble on the Middle Fork.

Appendix B

Information Sources

Ada County Parks and Waterways
Barber Park Office
208-343-1328

Bogus Basin Ski Area
2405 Bogus Basin Rd.
Boise, ID 83702
208-332-5100

Boise Parks and Recreation
1104 Royal Blvd.
Boise, ID 83706-2898
208-384-4240

Bureau of Land Management
Boise District Office
3948 Development Ave.
Boise, ID 83705
208-384-3300

Ridge to Rivers Trails Coordinator
208-384-3360

Ridge to Rivers Trails Hotline
208-384-4044

Idaho Department of Fish and Game
600 S. Walnut
Boise, ID 83707
208-334-3700

Southwest Idaho Mountain Bicycling Association
P.O. Box1443
Boise, ID 83701
208-377-7216

U.S. Forest Service
Boise Front Office
5493 Warm Springs Ave.
Boise, ID 83712
208-367-9320

Bike Shops

Bikes2Boards
28th & Sunset
Boise, ID 83702
208-343-0208

Bob's Bicycles
6112 Fairview Ave.
Boise, ID 83704
208-332-8042

Capitol Schwinn Cyclery
1015 Vista Ave.
Boise, ID 83705
208-336-2453

**George's Cycles
and Fitness**
1738 W. State St.
Boise, ID 83702
208-343-5677

Idaho Mountain Touring
1310 Main St.
Boise, ID 83702
208-336-3854

**Intermountain Outdoor
Sports**
1375 E. Fairview Ave.
Meridian, ID
208-888-4911

Ken's Bicycle Warehouse
10470 W. Overland Rd.
Boise, ID 83709
208-376-9240

McU Sports
822 W. Jefferson
Boise, ID 83702
200-342 7734

Moo Cycles
1517 1/2 N. 13th St.
(Hyde Park)
Boise, ID 83702
208-336-5229

Pedersen's Ski and Sports
350 N. Milwaukee
Boise Town Square Mall 83788
208-323-9381

**Recreational
Equipment Inc. (REI)**
8300 W. Emerald St.
Boise, ID 83704
208-322-1141

Spoke N Wheel
6815 Fairview Ave.
Boise, ID 83704
208-377-2091

Screamin' Toad Cycles
3115 N. State St.
Boise, ID
208-367-1899

World Cycle
180 N. 8th St.
Boise, ID 83702
208-343-9130

Glossary

ATB: All-terrain bicycle; a.k.a. mountain bike, sprocket rocket, fat tire flyer.

ATV: All-terrain vehicle; in this book ATV refers to motorbikes and 3- and 4-wheelers designed for off-road use. See ORV below.

Bedrock: Rock that's fixed to the earth, immobile.

Bail: Getting off the bike, usually in a hurry, and whether or not you mean to. Often a last resort.

Bunny hop: Leaping up, while riding, and lifting both wheels off the ground to jump over an obstacle (or for sheer joy).

Clean: To ride without touching a foot (or other body part) to the ground; to ride a tough section successfully.

Contour: A line on a topographic map showing a continuous elevation level over uneven ground. Also used as a verb to indicate a fairly easy or moderate grade: "The trail contours around the west flank of the mountain before the final grunt to the top."

Dab: To put a foot or hand down (or hold onto or lean on a tree or other support) while riding. If you have to dab, then you haven't ridden that piece of trail **clean.**

Dip: A short drop followed by a quick rise in a trail. Most dips can be surmounted by momentum, skill, and previous knowledge of the terrain.

Downfall: Trees that have fallen across the trail, same as windfall.

Doubletrack: A trail, jeep road, ATV route, or other track with 2 distinct ribbons of **tread,** typically with grass growing in between.

No matter which side you choose, the other rut always looks smoother.

Endo: Lifting the rear wheel off the ground and riding (or abruptly not riding) on the front wheel only. Also known, at various degrees of control and finality, as a nose wheelie, "going over the handlebars," and a face plant.

Fall line: The angle and direction of a slope; the **line** you follow when gravity is in control and you aren't.

Fork: Although "fork" can refer to your front wheel cradle, the term in this book refers to a split or junction in the trail, usually at an acute angle. Can also be used as a verb.

Full-sprung: A bike with both front and rear suspension.

Goatheads: Goathead thorns, also called puncture vine. A ground-hugging annual with a nasty, multi-faceted thorn (up to 1/2" long). Mostly located near creek bottoms and most dangerous during the dry season when the heads are dry and hard; they are hard to spot. Look for small yellow blossoms mid to late summer. See **Slime**.

Granny gear: The innermost and smallest of the three chain rings on the bottom bracket spindle (where the pedals and crank arms attach to the bike's frame). Shift down to your granny gear (and up to the biggest cog on the rear hub) to find your lowest (easiest) gear for climbing.

Grunt: A sustained steep hill, usually not very enjoyable. An entire ride can be referred to as a grunt.

Hoodoo: A rock outcropping, larger than a person and more vertically proportioned than a boulder.

Kelly hump: An abrupt mound of dirt across the road or trail. These are common on old logging roads and skidder tracks, placed there to block vehicle access and to divert water. At high speeds, they become launching pads for bikes and freefall warriors.

Line: The route (or trajectory) between or over obstacles or through turns. **Tread** or trail refers to the ground you're riding on; the line is the path you choose within the tread (and exists mostly in the eye of the beholder).

Off-the-seat: Moving your butt behind the bike seat and over the rear tire; used for control on extremely steep descents. This position increases braking power, helps prevent **endos,** and reduces skidding.

ORV: Off-Road Vehicle; any motorized vehicle designed for tearing up the dirt. Akin to ATV above.

Outrig: To dab, especially on a thin sidehill trail.

Portage: To carry the bike, usually up a steep hill, across unrideable obstacles, or through a stream.

Quads: Thigh muscles (short for quadricep); or maps in the USGS topographic series (short for quadrangles). Nice quads of either kind can help get you out of trouble in the backcountry.

Ratcheting: Also known as backpedaling; rotating the pedals backwards to avoid hitting them on rocks or other obstacles.

Rollers/rolling: A section of trail that undulates (rises and falls) repetitively. Frequency and modulation can vary greatly.

Shutterbumps: A washboard surface, usually on a sand/gravel road. They also make you "shudder" off your handlebars if speed is not properly checked.

Sidehill: Where the trail crosses a slope. If the **tread** is narrow, keep your inside (uphill) pedal up to avoid hitting the ground. If the tread tilts downhill, you may have to use some body language to keep the bike plumb or vertical to avoid slipping out.

Singletrack: A trail, game run, or other track with only one ribbon of **tread.** Good singletrack is pure fun.

Slimer: A green mucus-looking liquid used inside tire tubes to seal small punctures. Found in bike shops all over the Boise area.

Spur: A side road or trail that splits off from the main route, also split or fork.

Surf: Riding through loose gravel or sand, when the wheels sway from side to side. Also *heavy surf:* frequent and difficult obstacles.

Suspension: A bike with front suspension has a shock-absorbing fork or stem. Rear suspension absorbs shock between the rear wheel and frame. A bike with both is said to be fully suspended.

Switchbacks: When a trail goes up a steep slope, it zig zags or *switchbacks* across the **fall line** to ease the gradient of the climb. Well-designed switchbacks make a turn with at least an 8-foot radius and remain fairly level within the turn itself. These are rare, however, and cyclists often struggle to ride through sharply angled, sloping switchbacks.

Tread: The riding surface, particularly regarding **singletrack.**

Water bar: A log, rock, or other barrier placed in the **tread** to divert water off the trail and prevent erosion. In the Boise Front water bars tend to be black neoprene skirts embedded in the soil, looking like auto tire sidewalls with slices in them.

WCO: World Class Obstacle. A large or especially tricky problem in the trail that requires portaging to surmount (for mortals). WCOs can be found in lower Hulls Gulch and lower Crane Creek trails. Technical rating is 5+.

Zoomer: A smooth, downhill, section of a ride. Although fun, zoomers present great danger to the rider and others. A true zoomer affords excellent visibility.

A Short Index of Rides

Road Rides
(includes paved pathways and mixed routes)
1. Hidden Springs Loop (1 to 3+) 6.3 miles
2. Seamans Gulch-Dry Creek (1 to 2) 10.6 miles
3. Greenbelt West (1 to 5) 7 miles
8. Cartwright–Pierce Park (1 to 2) 11.5 miles
9. Cartwright–Dry Creek (1 to 2) 17.4 miles
7. Boise Greenbelt–Oregon Trail (1 to 3+) 27.1 miles
22. Barber–Warm Springs Loop (1) 7.6 miles

Easier Technical Rides
(may also include road and doubletrack)

4. Quail–Harrison Hollows (1 to 3+) 4.9 miles
5. Stewart Gulch Loop (1 to 3) 5.9 miles
14. Highland–8th St.–Camelback (1 to 3+) 4.9 miles
15. Crestline–Mountain Cove Loop (1 to 3+) 6.3 miles
20. Rocky Canyon Road (1 to 2) 13 miles
23. Castle Rock Loop (1 to 3) 2.7 miles
37. Lower Nordic Loop (1 to 3+) 4.1 miles

Intermediate Technical

6. Hillside–Harrison Hollow Ridge (1 to 4) 5 miles
10. Crane Creek–Corrals Loop (1 to 5) 9.9 miles
11. Corrals–8th St. Loop (1 to 4+) 12 miles

16. Eagle Ridge Loop (2 to 5) 5.1 miles
17. 8th St.–Scott's Trail Loop (2 to 4) 6.4 miles
18. Hulls Gulch–Crestline Trail (1 to 4+) 7.7 miles
21. Crestline–Sidewinder Loop (1 to 4+) 8.6 miles
24. Table Rock Lower Loop (1 to 5) 4.9 miles
25. Table Rock Loop (2 to 4) 5.3 miles
26. Castle Rock–Table Rock Loop (2 to 5) 6.2 miles
31. Curlew Ridge Loop (1 to 5) 6.4 miles
32. Lower Curlew Ridge Loop (1 to 5) 7.1 miles
36. Shafer Butte Loop (1 to 4) 12.8 miles
38. Elk Meadows (1 to 4) 4.1 miles
39. Mores Mountain Loop (2 to 5) 4.6 miles
40. Sappers Return Loop (2 to 4) 4.8 miles

Serious Rides

(includes longer and more technical routes)

12. Hulls Gulch–Crane Creek Loop (1 to 5) 9.2 miles
13. Lucky Peak Loop (1 to 3+) 25.3 miles
19. Crestline-Curlew Ridge Loop (2 to 4+) 15.7 miles
27. West Highland Valley–Cobb Trail Loop (1 to 4)
    6.7 miles
28. Squaw Creek–Cobb Trail Loop (1 to 4) 8.1 miles
29. Highland Valley–Squaw Creek Loop (1 to 4+)
    9.9 miles
30. Highland Valley–Lucky Peak Dam Loop (2 to 4+)
    10.2 miles
33. Boise Ridge–Deer Point Loop (1 to 4) 25.3 miles
34. 8th St. High Loop (2 to 5) 11.6 miles
35. Shingle Creek Ridge Loop (1 to 4+) 14.4 miles

About the Author

Martin Potucek has lived, climbed, skied, and biked in Idaho since 1972. His background as a cultural revolutionist on a commune near Sandpoint eventually led to his current occupation as an independent contractor in design and construction in Boise. He has also taught and practiced professional and technical writing from one end of the state to the other. Among his current projects is a guide to the trails of the Spokane–Coeur d'Alene area.

FALCON GUIDES ®Leading the Way™

MOUNTAIN BIKING GUIDES

Mountain Biking Arizona
Mountain Biking Colorado
Mountain Biking Georgia
Mountain Biking Idaho
Mountain Biking New York
Mountain Biking N. New England
Mountain Biking North Carolina
Mountain Biking Oregon
Mountain Biking Pennsylvania
Mountain Biking South Carolina
Mountain Biking Southern California
Mountain Biking S. New England
Mountain Biking Utah
Mountain Biking Washington
Mountain Biking Wisconsin
Mountain Biking Wyoming
The Mountain Biker's Guide to New Mexico

BIRDING GUIDES

Birding Georgia
Birding Illinois
Birding Minnesota
Birding Montana
Birding Northern California
Birding Texas
Birding Utah

FISHING GUIDES

Fishing Alaska
Fishing the Beartooths
Fishing Florida
Fishing Glacier
Fishing Maine
Fishing Montana
Fishing Wyoming
Fishing Yellowstone National Park
Trout Unlimited's Guide to America's
    100 Best Trout Streams
Trout Unlimited's Guide to Amercia's 50
    Best Bass Waters

LOCAL CYCLING SERIES

Mountain Biking Albuquerque
Mountain Biking Bend
Mountain Biking Boise
Mountain Biking Chequamegon
Mountain Biking Chico
Mountain Biking Colorado Springs
Mountain Biking Denver/Boulder
Mountain Biking Durango
Mountain Biking Flagstaff and Sedona
Mountain Biking Grand Junction
    and Fruita
Mountain Biking Helena
Mountain Biking Moab
Mountain Biking Phoenix
Mountain Biking Spokane &
    Coeur d'Alene
Mountain Biking the Twin Cities
Mountain Biking Utah's
    St. George/Cedar City Area
Mountain Biking White
    Mountains (West)

PADDLING GUIDES

Paddling Minnesota
Paddling Montana
Paddling Okefenokee
Paddling Oregon
Paddling Yellowstone/Grand Teton

ROCKHOUNDING GUIDES

Rockhounding Arizona
Rockhounding California
Rockhounding Colorado
Rockhounding Montana
Rockhounding Nevada
Rockhound's Guide to New Mexico
Rockhounding Texas
Rockhounding Utah
Rockhounding Wyoming

To order check with you local bookseller or
call FALCON® at **1-800-582-2665**.
www.falcon.com

FALCON®

FALCON GUIDES ®Leading the Way™

All books in this popular series are regularly updated with accurate information on access, side trips, & safety.

FALCON®